CAJUN NAVY
GROUND FORCE

CAJUN NAVY GROUND FORCE
Citizen-Led Disaster Response

By Rob Gaudet

PELICAN PUBLISHING
New Orleans

*The word "Pelican" and the depiction of a pelican are
trademarks of Arcadia Publishing Company Inc. and are
registered in the U.S. Patent and Trademark Office.*

Library of Congress Cataloging-in-Publication Data

Names: Gaudet, Rob, author.
Title: cajun navy ground force : citizen-led disaster response / Rob Gaudet.
Description: New Orleans : Pelican Publishing, 2022. | Summary: " Cajun
  Navy Ground Force recounts the origin of the Cajun Navy Foundation
  and its efforts to provide disaster relief during the Louisiana flooding
  of 2016 and beyond. The author also details his leadership role and the
  group's national profile"— Provided by publisher.
Identifiers: LCCN 2021062888 | ISBN 9781455625734 (trade paperback) |
  ISBN 9781455625741 (ebook)
Subjects: LCSH: Disaster relief—Louisiana. | Emergency management—
  Louisiana. | Hurricanes—Louisiana. | Floods—Louisiana. | Voluntarism—
  Louisiana.
Classification: LCC HV555.U62 L632 2022 | DDC 363.34/809763—dc23/
  eng/20220621
LC record available at https://lccn.loc.gov/2021062888

Printed in the United States of America

Published by Pelican Publishing
New Orleans, LA
www.pelicanpub.com

Contents

Acknowledgments

Thank you to the Cajun Navy Ground Force's board of directors:
Pat Miller
James Wood
Sheila Pritchett

Thank you to all of our team leads:
Stacy Parker
Jay Carter
Michelle Szinaval
Barbra Dykman
Lori Kirkpatrick
Shane Callcut
Jennifer Jagneaux
Chad Chiasson
Kevin Harper
Sheila Searcy
Earl D. Roe, Jr.
Jimmy O. Tarbell II
Matthew Dower
Kat Lubinski
Pete Sterk
Coby Leftwich
Tim Johnson
Alek Goldbronn

And thank you to all of the thousands of volunteers who have shown up. Thank you all for being there for the right reasons and for seeing the vision that shaped the Cajun Navy Ground Force. You have all donated your time and talents. Your hard work and dedication mean more than you will ever know. You have been through the fire with me and stuck with it.

This book is dedicated to you.

Thank you to Lori Kirkpatrick, who really helped me by transcribing my words to create this manuscript.

Finally, I'd like to thank my special person, my girlfriend, Camille Domingue. Camille has assisted with editing, letter writing, phone calls, volunteer management, and so much more. She has stood by my side through the often hard times of the Cajun Navy Ground Force's efforts, as well as through the process of writing this book. She makes sure I eat and sleep and breathe, and she loves me. She is my world. I'm grateful for that fateful day, 02/02/2020, when we met. Without her, this would not get done.

CAJUN NAVY
GROUND FORCE

Chapter 1

The Storm with No Name

You open your front door to see that the roads have disappeared. As far as your eyes can see, there is nothing but mailbox-high water. The next thing you know, your child, wife, and pets are standing on the kitchen table, with water just about to the top of the table and still rising. In that moment, your mind starts racing, and it seems as if the world is ending. What about your wife's elderly parents in a neighborhood not far away? What about your wife's car and your truck? What about your job? When will the water recede?

What feels like an hour is actually only seconds. You turn back to look at your family standing on the kitchen table. In only seconds, the water has risen another foot, and your eight-year-old daughter is crying. She now has water up to her knees. It's time to do something, and fast.

With water still rising, you swim out of your front door to your car in your driveway and climb on top of it to take a look around. South Louisiana is a sportsman's paradise. Duck hunting and fishing are our favorite outdoor pastimes, so boats are everywhere. Looking across the street at your neighbors' driveway, you see their flat-bottom boat floating in the brown swirling water.

They're on vacation. You half-wade, half-swim to their house through a swift-moving current carrying debris, fire ants, gas, and chemicals, and you commandeer the craft. Climbing in, you realize it's not fresh rainwater you were in. It's brimming with garbage, sewage, and animals both dead and alive, including snakes. The water itself is dangerous and it's rising on your family.

Your adrenaline is pumping, and you move fast. The boat has a motor but it won't start without a key, so you grab the oar sitting in the bottom and paddle into your garage. Then you jump back into the quagmire and fetch your daughter off the table. Your wife is holding your dog, but where is your cat? No time to think about it. You keep your daughter lifted above your head so she's out of the water. Your wife hops into the water next to you and you all make your way to the boat.

You hear a motor outside, and it's a friend from a few streets over. His boat has his family and your wife's parents in it. He pulls up and hops out to help you load your wife and child into his boat. He tells your wife that he saw her post on Facebook begging someone to check on her parents, and they are OK.

As you're thinking about where to go, your wife says that according to what she's been reading on Facebook, you must get to the I-10 overpass. There are troops and first responders on standby there with high-water vehicles to drive you to a shelter. Your friend drives the boat to the drop-off point, where you both unload your human cargo. That's when you notice a flotilla of citizen boats coming and going, all loaded with people and pets and possessions.

Your wife tells you what she saw on Facebook. Everyone is working together through technology, using social media and mobile apps. She advises you to download the walkie-talkie app Zello and get on the Cajun Navy Disaster Response channel, so that you can go help others. She also tells you to download the GPS app Glympse, so citizen dispatchers working from home and taking in rescue requests can see on a map if you're close to someone needing help.

You download both of the apps, turn them on, and hear the crackle of the walkie-talkie. A stranger calls your Zello handle and asks, "Do you copy?" You press the button on the app and respond, "Copy." The citizen dispatcher replies immediately, "You are half a mile from a recent request. I need you to go pick up a family of six that is stranded on their roof. There are two dogs, two adults, a senior, and three small children. I texted you their address. Please check in with me when you arrive. I'll be tracking your movements through the GPS app. Please be safe."

You respond with a confirmation and load the address into your GPS app. You and your buddy take off to do your first rescue.

This is the Cajun Navy.

A Technology-Based Operation

This intensely destructive weather was occurring during the 2016 Olympics and the Trump vs. Clinton presidential campaigns. It was not a tropical depression. It did not come off the Gulf of Mexico, where Louisiana storms usually form. It didn't have a name. This massive, fearsome rain system formed and lingered for about four days over my home in St. Francisville to the east and Alexandria to the west.

Lake Pontchartrain, an estuary north of New Orleans, was far to the east of the rain. It is somewhat oval in shape, covering an area of 630 square miles with an average depth of twelve to fourteen feet. About 40 miles from west to east and 24 miles from south to north, it is spanned by the world's longest continuous bridge. The rain that started falling that fateful week in the middle of August filled up all of the bayous, creeks, streams, and rivers in the central region of the state with enough water to fill Lake Pontchartrain four times. These rivers and bayous and creeks swelled up and overflowed, their waters flooding everything as they moved south toward the gulf.

Nobody saw it coming. It rains here all the time, and flooding is fairly normal. We have localized flooding in the streets pretty often, but I had never seen anything like this in my life. Nobody expected that their homes were going to be inundated, but it happened.

As the water rose through dozens of unsuspecting cities, towns, and neighborhoods that had never flooded before, this scene played out over and over from August 13 to August 18, 2016. People found themselves stranded in floodwater with no way out. No first-response organization could have been prepared for the tens of thousands who needed rescue. So stranded citizens went to Facebook, seeking assistance.

My role in all of this? I recognized that the rescue requests on Facebook were not being responded to in any organized manner. Therefore, I organized the effort, by training people working from home to track the requests for help and asking others to dispatch.

Volunteers working from their kitchen tables took many hundreds of urgent requests coming through the Cajun Navy Emergency Operations Facebook group. They used a couple of mobile apps to coordinate an enormous ground force who climbed into their own boats, borrowed boats, or commandeered boats, then received their dispatch orders to rescue people, pets, and possessions from floodwaters.

Helping Neighbors

My introduction to the Cajun Navy came after my buddy, Chris Pilie, and I went out to see what we could do to help some of his neighbors during the 2016 flood. He lived in Prairieville, a small community on Airline Highway, right in the heart of where the worst flooding was occurring.

As I turned off Airline Highway to get to Chris's neighborhood, I glanced down to see that the water was halfway up the door of my truck. I was keenly aware of the deep ditches on either side of the road, now hidden by water. I inched along to Chris's house, which managed not to flood even though the murky waters surrounded it. I waited as Chris sloshed toward my truck in slow motion.

Chris and I both have always maintained a significant social-media presence. His was for his radio program in New Orleans and mine for political activism. As we set out to explore the flooded area that day, we started to document the experience on Facebook Live. During one of these videos, we were heading down this road not far from Chris's house.

You could see that the water was concealing the road, but we decided to venture a little farther. Once we reached some dry land, we hopped out to take a look. Boats were arriving, and people were coming and going along the inundated path almost as though this were normal.

We could not help but notice one particular house off to the right. It was evident that the water was not yet in the woman's house, but it was covering the floor of her carport. My eyes were drawn to an RV and some other random items under her carport, including a folding table that stood in the middle of the uninvited water. There was some food on the table, as if she was enjoying a picnic.

As we stood there, caught somewhat off guard, the woman approached us, a full bowl cupped in each hand.

"Do y'all want some gumbo?" she pressed.

Was this real? How could someone in the midst of their own personal suffering be concerned about whether or not we, perfect strangers, have had lunch? Yet there she stood, in the process of losing everything, cooking gumbo on a burner that was partially submerged in the water. I suppose this act of kindness for her neighbors, this offer of some semblance of hope, was what was carrying her through the chaos around her.

I watched in awe as people wandered up through the floodwaters. The seemingly unshaken woman was greeting them from her flooded driveway with gumbo and a smile on her face. Many accepted both with gratitude.

"Do y'all want to come sit down?" she asked us expectantly.

Her name was Ms. Barbara, we learned. We continued standing there on dry concrete on the side of the road.

"At the table? In the water?" I asked, glancing over at Chris.

Chris just looked at me, shrugging his shoulders.

"OK, why not?!" I decided.

Still filming on Facebook Live, I pointed the camera down at my feet. I somehow knew that this was the beginning of something. I was not sure what, but I knew it had touched me and would change me forever. I could not quite put my finger on it at the time, but in retrospect I can see without a doubt that this was a defining moment. It was my debut, my entry into the Cajun Navy.

OK, here we go, I breathed.

"Chris, we just have to talk to the people coming out," I said.

Water was inching into the house next to Ms. Barbara's. The couple made their way out of their home, carrying boxes of papers, photographs, and other mementos that they did not want to lose. We talked with them for a while on Facebook Live, and during that conversation, we asked if they needed anything. Not long after we chatted with them, I edged toward the water. With dry shoes, socks, and shorts, I decided to wade over to their house. It was a baptism of sorts.

The couple had some other people with them. They were all standing around, and one of them announced that they were waiting for sandbags. Suddenly, some guys pulled up in a truck loaded with sandbags, and we helped unload them and stack them around the house. We were all hoping to slow the intrusion of the water.

"Where did you get those sandbags?" I asked. "We want to go there."

The guys gave us directions to a middle school, so we jumped into my truck and headed over to help fill sandbags. It was not far and we were able to make it there without any trouble. When we arrived, we spotted a crowd of people filling bags from a gigantic pile of sand. I saw a face that I thought I recognized.

"Is that David Duke filling sandbags?" I asked.

Surprisingly, it was him. I remembered when he ran for governor of Louisiana in 1991. He was a former Grand Wizard of the KKK. It felt so odd to be standing beside this blatant bigot who once ran for the top office in the state, filling sandbags that would be destined for all races. I went back to my truck, turned my truck's camera on, and pointed it at the sandbag pile as we continued our work.

There was a moment when it occurred to me that it did not matter who you were. We were all in the same proverbial boat and just wanted to do something, anything, to help in this seemingly hopeless situation. Still, that fleeting thought didn't remove the bad taste in my mouth from being so close to him, so I just focused on shoveling sand.

When there was no more sand, we decided to contact the authorities to see if we could go help somewhere else. I looked up the number for the city of Gonzales and called.

It only rang once. A voice said quickly, "Gonzales City Hall. This is the mayor speaking." The mayor was overwhelmed; we could hear it. He told us where we could go to help. Unfortunately, it was the same place we had just been, filling sandbags. We explained that there was no more sand, and he replied that he didn't have anything else for us to do. But it just did not seem as though we were doing enough. There should have been something we could do on a larger scale.

As I brought Chris home, we decided to film the rising floodwaters. I pulled over, and Chris got out of the truck and started to walk. He broadcast live while I drove behind him. By this time, it was about six at night, so after a few minutes of filming, Chris got back in the truck.

I dropped him off at his house and left. Interstate 10, a major route through the area, had flooded in Baton Rouge and been shut down. Traffic was being redirected onto Airline Highway, creating a major bottleneck for thousands, including me. What normally was a five-minute drive up two lanes of highway took seven hours.

During that time, I filmed on Facebook Live multiple times. As I crept along, the sound of sirens permeated the air. Several times, I watched in my rearview mirror as cars moved to each side of the highway to make room for police and ambulances. It looked like the parting of the Red Sea. As the emergency vehicles approached, I took my turn pulling to the side.

Eventually, around midnight, as I progressed toward the end of the backup, I realized what was slowing us down. I could just barely see the guardrails in the darkness, but the road was completely invisible. Only the Bayou Manchac sign told me where I was. I was on a bridge, on a highway, and all I could see was water.

These are the places the authorities warn you about. Yet here we were, thousands of vehicles making their way over a flooded bridge. I had only one option. I closely followed the car in front of me, to make sure I did not go off into the bayou. Car after car followed the taillights in front of them, and it was the blind leading the blind. I was videoing this, and at some point I have to admit that I freaked out a bit. I turned off my camera; maybe subconsciously I didn't want my final moments broadcast on Facebook Live.

Aware of the danger, I needed undisturbed concentration. The car I had been following came to an abrupt halt, but the vehicle ahead of it continued on. That is not good, I thought, until I realized that the one in front of me finally started inching along once again.

I simply could not distinguish if I was on the highway, or close to the edge of the bridge, or worse, near one of the deep ditches that lined the roadside. I made up my mind that I would keep following the car in front of me, and if it went into a ditch, then I would just stop. It was an intense and stressful drive. I breathed a sigh of relief once I made it over the bridge and finally arrived at home.

The following day, I was watching TV when I heard on the news about a group called the Cajun Navy. A reporter was live at a movie studio in Baton Rouge that had been converted to a shelter. As she spoke in front of the building, you could see behind her a helicopter that had recently landed. The people who had just been dropped off, rescued from the floodwaters, were wandering around in disbelief, then walking toward the shelter.

The reporter hurried over and gripped one of the guys on his arm. "Hey, would you tell us about what just happened?" she asked.

The man, who had just stepped out of the helicopter, turned to the camera looking like a deer caught in headlights. He was on the verge of tears and mumbled while looking around nervously, "I just lost everything. My car is under water; I do not know if I have a job; I don't know where my family is."

With that, he stumbled away from the camera without saying another word.

That poignant moment made it all unmistakably real for me. I was so moved by the man's words that I could not get them out of my mind. I did not have water in my home but it was very close, probably a foot away. Before long, I could be in the same situation as the man on TV.

I went outside and tried to measure the rising water in front of my home. Was it still coming up? I sat on my front porch and tried to relax with my dog, Nola. I threw her ball, and she happily retrieved it in the newly formed lake surrounding our house. She naturally loves water, so she was running and jumping off the porch into the flood, swimming for the ball, and bringing it back to me. I decided to get on Facebook to see what was new. I was just scrolling along when I saw that name again—this thing called the Cajun Navy that I had heard about on the news earlier.

I searched and found the Facebook group, and I joined it without much consideration. I wanted to see what this group was up to. Right away, it was evident to me that this flooding was big. Many people were asking to be rescued, and I could see that members of the group were responding to their calls for help. However, it was not coordinated at all.

It was clear to me that nobody was in charge of this operation. It was very ad hoc. Without a second thought, I messaged the group administrator and explained to her that I made my living using Facebook. I wrote that I had been pretty successful at it, and I was sure I could help her organize the rescues.

She did not even take time to respond to my message. She simply made me a group administrator on the spot. I messaged her again and said, "Look, let's talk real quick. I have some things that I would like to do." She told me to go ahead with my plan. She explained that she was just another volunteer and somebody in the group had made her an administrator before they disappeared. It appeared to me that this was an abandoned group that was just growing on its own.

As soon as I logged into the group as an admin, I changed the home image to something eye catching and came up with a hashtag that would make it easy to find by people needing help. Then I noticed the thing I kept hearing people talk about—Zello, a walkie-talkie app. I picked up my phone and searched for it. When I found the channel that was created for the Cajun Navy, I hopped on and started engaging with listeners. I explained that I was in the Facebook group, and we had people who needed to be rescued.

"Is there anybody out there that can help?" I asked.

Chapter 2

An Outpouring of Support

There was an overwhelming response from the followers on Zello. I realized right away that this operation was going to be way more involved than I could handle by myself, so I began asking for people in the group to jump in. Next I created a Google Docs spreadsheet to organize the information. I put out an all-call for volunteers to help gather the requests, and I added the requests to the spreadsheet. This would allow us to share the information with each other and provide it to boaters to go out and do rescues.

The rescues continued almost nonstop for the following ten days, but there was still so much more to be done. I was renting an office in Baton Rouge at the time, so I got used to sleeping in the apartment upstairs. I did not even think about going home that whole time. We continued coordinating rescues, and the media intently monitored the activity in the Facebook group. It wasn't long before they started calling and texting me. They wanted me to appear on their shows and talk about what our group was doing to help.

In the middle of all this, a woman originally from the Baton Rouge area friended me. She was now living in Dallas, working for a U.S. representative from Texas. I thought, *Wow, somebody with influence is watching what we are doing.* The press had not been covering this huge disaster very much at that point. Nearly 150,000 homes had flooded, but that barely made the national news. It was simply a side story. It did not make sense to me, although it was easy to see which other stories were stealing the spotlight.

It was the end of the Summer Olympics, and the presidential campaigns between Donald Trump and Hillary Clinton were getting all of the news coverage. I did everything I could to gain the attention of the press, and thankfully, this woman became a tremendous help with that. I was able to appear on the radio shows of Rush Limbaugh and Sean Hannity to talk about what we were doing. I was also interviewed on Fox News Radio by Sandra Smith. The Dallas woman really opened a bunch of doors for me and brought recognition to the Cajun Navy Ground Force during a time when we needed it most. She and I found that we had a lot of friends in common.

More media started reaching out, telling us that they had seen our group on Facebook, CNN, the Weather Channel, and other outlets.

All of this happened in a relatively short time, approximately two weeks. It was a whirlwind. I was lucky to work remotely at the time for a company out of Shreveport. I had been with them for three years, building a software platform. I called my boss and told him that I was helping with this disaster, if it was OK with him. Thankfully, I had his complete support, and he encouraged me to carry on.

When the flooding had gone down, and all the rescues were completed, the volunteers remained committed and wanted to keep helping. However, we were not quite sure what we could do next. At the same time, I knew that I needed to get back to work. It was heart wrenching, and I was torn by the dilemma.

The last thing I wanted was to just turn my back and walk away from all of this momentum that had been created. Most of all, I did not want to walk away from the people. It was definitely a movement, and you do not just walk away from that. In order to keep things rolling, I turned to two guys who coordinated the boats. The three of us collaborated and became the organizers of the whole movement.

I asked one of the other organizers if he wanted to participate in an interview with the Fox Business channel. He lives in New Orleans and it was closer for him, so it made sense for him to take that opportunity. However, he was not comfortable with being on television, so I ended up rushing over to do the interview at four o'clock in the morning. It was too big of an opportunity to pass up.

While waiting to be interviewed, I was also asked to appear on the Walton & Johnson radio show. I went on Fox Business for the interview, and I was surprised by how well it went. This was my first time on live television. And I have to admit, it was an intimidating experience. I was so tired that day, but I think I had so much adrenaline from the events of the past few weeks that the first live interview turned out to be effortless and rewarding.

However, I realized that urgent needs remained, and the system for providing help was just as overwhelmed as it was during the actual rescues. Here we were three weeks in, and we were all still going hard at it. We decided to help direct the supplies that were flowing into the area. We searched for which shelters needed water, food, diapers, or bathroom essentials. We directed logistics for citizens bringing donations into the

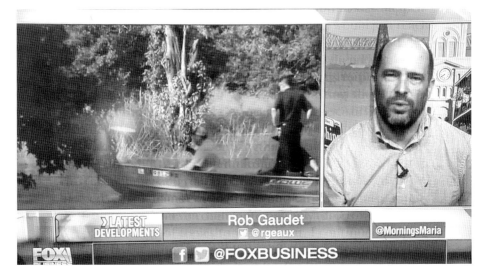

Rob Gaudet appearing on live national television to discuss the disaster response

city and directed volunteers to distribute them to various shelters. We stayed busy trying to make sure we were sending the supplies where they were needed the most.

Once during this time, I drove a truck for nine hours with a friend to Jacksonville, Florida, because people were setting up remote collection centers in other states. We went to a huge warehouse of donated supplies, filled up the truck, and drove it back to a shelter in Baton Rouge. This trip enabled me to see that this was not just a local effort. Communities outside of the state were actively helping, as well.

The next morning, the team was preparing to get online and keep coordinating relief efforts and supplies with the 20,000 others who had joined the group in the previous weeks. I opened my laptop, launched Facebook, and tried to go into the Cajun Navy group like always. But to my surprise, one of the volunteers with admin rights had removed the access of the other admins. We were shocked. What the heck just happened?

This volunteer had not been active with the Cajun Navy for weeks. There was no communication from him about this access change. This person, who now runs a Cajun Navy group of a different flavor, had hijacked the Cajun Navy group that my team built. We still had countless people in need who were reaching out to me, wanting assistance that could only be provided through the coordinated efforts of our group. So at this point, I founded a 501(c)(3) nonprofit organization and I named it Cajun Relief Foundation.

Many people showed up to help out in whatever ways we could find. We were able to locate many families who were essentially on the fringes and absolutely needed our help. It was rewarding to know that we were assisting so many people during that season of their lives. They had lost everything— their cars, their homes, and all of their possessions. Their homes could be repaired but needed to be cleaned out. So we focused on what we could do, and we did it.

Thoughts of those who had no money or insurance haunted me. I knew that no one was assisting them, so my team and I went to help. One such family was Miss Donna and her eighty-year-old mother, Theresa. Donna, though paralyzed from the neck down, is an artist who skillfully uses her mouth to draw and paint her masterpieces. We asked her to create a Cajun Navy painting that we could use to raise funds; she agreed.

Once it was done, we sold it through our website for fifty dollars per print. We raised $2,500 for her from that single campaign. We held another fundraiser for Donna and Theresa where we found a popular local band that was willing to donate their time to perform. We raised another $2,500 for this family.

It took the two women two and a half years to get back into their home. While waiting to return home, Donna, who lived in a windowless room in the back of a FEMA trailer, never lost hope. She was a true inspiration to everyone who met them and even to those who simply heard their story. In that disaster, we were able to help Miss Donna and countless others in meaningful ways. We helped them get back on their feet.

It was baffling to me that people chose to go on with their everyday lives while there was so much need and so much destruction in their own community. This was happening before our very eyes. During this time, I realized that I had a valuable skill. Instead of giving 1 case of water, I could move 10,000 cases of water by engaging people on social media and recruiting them to volunteer. As we moved forward, that is how I chose to use my time.

Looking back on the Louisiana Flood of 2016, I know that we were able to use hundreds of boats to save thousands of people. But it was really technology that made it possible. Because of technology, we had dispatchers working at kitchen tables who could send boats to save people. Once the rescues were over, the effort didn't stop. Many of the Cajun Navy volunteers, fueled by adrenaline, soda, coffee, and a lack of sleep, assisted in the cleaning and gutting of houses and eventually the rebuilding efforts.

People were saying I had become the face of the Cajun Navy. I was invited to appear on national news broadcasts and give interviews to various publications. To my mind, however, I was only a cog in the wheel. I didn't seek or want attention or the limelight. It had all been a team effort. But I was glad to share what I had seen and encourage others to help. I saw the recognition as a means of bringing attention to a nameless disaster that, until that time, the media had largely ignored.

We as a team demonstrated how, in a flash, good citizens could get up, band together, and save people in their darkest hours. To further our efforts, we continued to streamline our technology and the tools that we used. Our objective has never been to compete with any of the other long-standing organizations. We set ourselves apart by utilizing technology to achieve outcomes, while doing the right things for the right reasons. Technology is what enables and changes the way citizens can engage in a time of disaster.

Sourcing resources and volunteers through social media was so successful that it became a movement. It wasn't just in Louisiana or even the United States. I knew that efforts such as this could be successful on a global scale. I was certain this model could work anywhere that had motivated citizens who care about each other and are willing to act together to help their neighbor in need.

I was reminded of my purpose and of the connectedness of humanity while I was doing flood relief at a home in Denham Springs. As I worked, I noticed a man walking with a violin. I was touched, initially because the beautiful instrument had clearly been ravaged by floodwaters.

Cajun Relief Foundation cofounder Melissa Wynn Adair was stuck working in Washington at that time. She and I have been a team for a long while on a variety of projects. I was aware, based on our communications, that she desperately wanted to be on the ground with us, working for the flood victims. In fact, she was distraught about being pulled away.

After watching the man amble toward the garbage pile with the violin in hand, I recalled that Melissa happened to be a trained violinist. What an interesting coincidence. I thought it would be nice to snap a photo of the instrument and send it to her, so I approached the gentleman and asked his permission. He obliged, and I took my photo.

The man with the tattered violin, Russell, and I began to talk, and he told me that he was there with a group of 6,000 Mormons. They had traveled to the area from Atlanta, Georgia for the purpose of assisting flood victims. I mentioned to Russell that I had a friend who was a Mormon from the Atlanta area, as well. I explained that she played the violin and her name was Melissa.

Surprised, Russell piped up and asked, "Do you mean Melissa Adair?"

I was shocked. "Uh, yeah! How do you know Melissa?"

Russell told me that Melissa had been his wife's best friend, but his wife had passed away from cancer. I choked up at this and asked in disbelief, "Was your wife named Kimberly?"

As both of us fought back tears, Russell responded, "Yes. . . . "

I told him I knew all about his wife's passing because Melissa had shared it with me years ago. Kimberly had been an inspiration to me because of the way she fought and loved life. I remembered everything I heard about her.

With those words, Russell leaned over and whispered into my ear, "Melissa is an angel." He straightened and, with a tear, said it again: "An angel." Then he turned and walked away.

Knowing how Melissa eased Kimberly's pain and does the same for everyone around her, I would agree with Russell; she's an angel. To have bumped into Russell, Kim's husband, carrying a violin at that very moment, was divine intervention.

As I write this, it is Kimberly Lowry's birthday, and even after her passing, it seems she is still touching people. Perhaps this story has two angels in it?

Chapter 3

Hurricanes Harvey and Irma

Harvey, a devastating Category 4 hurricane that made landfall in Texas and Louisiana in August 2017, caused catastrophic flooding in many dozens of communities and was responsible for more than one hundred deaths. The Cajun Navy Ground Force's first big opportunity to participate in recovery efforts after the 2016 Louisiana flooding was when Hurricane Harvey struck southeast Texas and the Houston area. We engaged in that disaster without dispatch software but with a spreadsheet instead, documenting more than 4,500 rescues. With each ensuing crisis, the CNGF would refine our process, becoming more and more proficient in using technology to assist survivors.

Soon after Harvey raged through Texas and Louisiana, Hurricane Irma was bearing down on the state of Florida. It was supposed to move directly up the middle of the Panhandle, and there was an evacuation order for the whole state. Traffic was backed up everywhere as millions of people scrambled to leave.

Irma made landfall as a Category 4 hurricane in the Florida Keys and struck southwestern Florida at Category 3 intensity. Irma, which caused 134 deaths and widespread devastation across the affected areas, was one of the strongest and costliest hurricanes on record in the Atlantic basin. Six million Florida residents evacuated coastal areas.

In advance of Hurricane Irma striking, US Sen. Marco Rubio of Florida called personally to ask me to organize citizen-led relief in his state immediately. We got about forty-five teams across the state ready to go. He also asked me if we would be willing to train Donald Trump's campaign team on disaster response. Across the state of Florida, quite a few of the presidential campaign field personnel were still in place in 2017. Rubio invited us to join a phone call with them, to explain how to use technology to perform rescues. We got on the phone with the crew and described how to do what we do.

We told them how, almost exclusively through technology, we empower citizens in disaster-affected areas to go out and help other people, as well as funnel assistance to them. We demonstrated how we use a spreadsheet to log people needing assistance. We add those survivors to the spreadsheet and share that information with our team in order to go find and directly help individuals. We instructed them on how to accept requests ("tickets") for help and then how to dispatch and organize volunteers on the ground using Zello.

Despite all of our training efforts, we had some issues with implementing our system. Frankly, Florida is an aging state. The people who work campaigns tend to be older, and those in the crew were in their sixties and seventies.

The campaign team was just not up to speed on technology, and it was interesting for us to come across that. I had kind of read it on that very first call. Many of the folks were confused about how to use Zello, which is a simple mobile walkie-talkie app, to connect with people and go help them. They had challenges just even locating the app to download it—much less turn it on, create an account, and use it. I could see quickly and clearly that they were going to have a hard time with this approach to disaster response.

So that was really interesting to realize that what we do depends on people who can easily adopt new technologies. We continued on with our training efforts, working with the campaign crew to show them what to do. However, in the end, they were unable to address the issues and implement the system. After the hurricane, we ended up going and essentially doing our own work across the state of Florida by finding our own sets of volunteers. We simply organized groups to hold drives for food, various supplies, and toys. Our team contacted some of the Home Depots in the state and asked them to donate supplies. That was quite a small operation, with only three volunteers on the ground, but it was effective.

Another volunteer, Nick, drove around the state, helping disaster survivors as he found them. As he located people who needed our help, we directed our other volunteers to go and do whatever was called for. Nick was a tech-savvy guy who was willing to stream on Facebook Live, which was of great importance to us because we like to drive engagement.

Nick had some great strengths. He cared deeply about the people he helped. But he was young and at times could be a bit of a hothead. I remember one of our behind-the-scenes volunteers in our Emergency Operations Center urgently calling me. He said that Nick had been streaming on Facebook Live when the police pulled him over for speeding. While still on Facebook, Nick made negative comments about the police department.

It just goes to show the importance of knowing who you are working with. We learned from that situation that we had to do background checks on individuals and also take a good hard look at their Facebook pages. But Nick was a really good guy, and he helped a lot of people. He was not afraid to show up wherever assistance was needed, whereas others might hesitate to enter neighborhoods that they thought might be unsafe. Nick traveled around in his little Toyota Corolla, and he was happy to just be out there helping people. We gave him some funds and paid for his gas and other necessities when he volunteered with us.

I recall another volunteer, who came down from Illinois after Irma. His name is Bill, and he was formerly in the military. Bill reached out to us on Facebook, and we ended up partnering with him and funding his efforts. I remember he showed up in his Jeep right after he told us he was coming. He did not waste any time—he just gassed up his vehicle and, in a flash, drove down with his dog.

Bill drove all the way down to the Florida Keys, and he

helped many people there in Big Pine. He would just barrel through and get things done. I think Bill was down there for six weeks. We rented him a truck, and he lived in a Red Cross shelter while he was there. Every day Bill would gather and hand out supplies, and we would give him whatever we could to distribute. He was quite effective.

After Irma, Hurricane Maria struck Puerto Rico. Nick hopped on a plane and helped alongside us out there, mostly with supply distribution. After a while, we lost track of him. That was OK, since we were finishing up our efforts there. The rest of us continued helping in Florida.

Chapter 4

Hurricanes Florence and Michael

Hurricane Florence

Hurricane Florence originated as a disturbance near the Southern Cabo Verde Islands in late August 2018. It fluctuated in intensity before increasing to a Category 4 hurricane on September 10, as it threatened the Eastern Seaboard. Florence made landfall near Wrightsville Beach, close to Wilmington, North Carolina, four days later as a Category 1 hurricane. But do not let the category fool you. This hurricane brought a massive storm surge and sustained winds of up to eighty-five miles per hour for four days straight.

Florence inundated North Carolina and South Carolina with torrential rain. It was the wettest storm ever to hit North Carolina, with a few locations measuring more than thirty inches of precipitation and creating a terrible domino effect. Once the rivers crested, the water moved downstream, wreaking havoc. Record flooding developed over the next several days along the Cape Fear River, destroying roads and damaging thousands of homes and businesses.

In the agricultural town of Burgaw, about thirty miles north of Wilmington, the swollen Northeast Cape Fear River and various creeks connected to it poured into streets and homes. I-40 and other key roadways from the town to surrounding communities were flooded and badly damaged, basically cutting the area off from resources. Local authorities performed swift-water rescues. Other Cajun Navy groups tried to enter the area without communicating with authorities and, as a result, were asked to leave.

Burgaw is the county seat of Pender County. Seventy percent of that county experienced substantial flooding. Burgaw's hospital was even forced to close, and a mobile hospital was put up in a Family Dollar parking lot. Two women gave birth in that parking lot, and others were treated there for storm-related injuries. Patients had to be flown in by helicopter because of the flooding in the area.

A reporter from the *New York Times* actually came and interviewed me personally about our efforts following Hurricane Florence. I was working remotely, and I remember that, honestly, it was very hard to organize volunteers. I was in Louisiana trying to recruit people on the ground in North Carolina who really had not heard much about the Cajun Navy. Connecting with people there who wanted to help was extremely difficult.

Our team was trying to get a Zello channel rolling with people on the ground, but introducing them to it was not easy, and we really had no resources to do that—outside of just trying to reach out through Facebook. We had one or two guys with boats in that area. I recall that one of them went out to deliver food and supplies to people who were stranded and did not want to evacuate their homes after the storm. They had no way to get resources.

A handful of others came, collected and distributed supplies, and helped with different efforts on the ground. We still took tickets on Zello, and we had our dispatch software rolling.

We really did not rescue many people during that time, but we did help with animal rescues. We had connected with several volunteers who also focused on relocating pets. Dogs, cats, horses, and all kinds of livestock were stranded in floodwaters at a farm in rural Pender County, and one of our roving volunteers was the first one there to assess the situation. It was one of the first times we went on Facebook Live in that area to get the word out about what we were doing.

Parts of Pender County remained completely cut off from

surrounding areas for weeks. The biggest problem was that people could not return to their homes. They were just stranded, and all they could do was wait it out.

One of the significant things I remember from Florence is that we became a hub for information on resources. We focused on getting those details out the best way we could—through social media and our Zello channel. This is not to say that our organization did not perform rescues, but our main contribution after Florence was to serve as an information clearinghouse.

As soon as we knew resources were coming in, we directed people to them. People mostly found us on Facebook as they were looking for information. As they discovered us, we provided more information there. I recall that we posted a lot of maps showing roads that were open and passable. We also let the public know where to find shelters, pet-friendly shelters, and distribution points for supplies.

County officials blocked some of the other groups from participating in any kind of first-responder efforts and even asked them to leave. One group accused us of standing at the end of their staging area and collecting donations using their identity, which was ridiculously false. I think one of their group had been a Cajun Relief volunteer after Hurricane Irma and was wearing one of our T-shirts, so someone took that and ran with it. I knew that we had never collected any donations in that area or from anything related to Florence.

We also had some problems with folks showing up and claiming that they were with us when they really were not. While we had some volunteers who became problems for us during that time, we also gained several who have stood with us and continue to take on major roles in our organization. Take Shane Callcut, for instance. Here is what he had to say about how he got his start with us.

"I started during Hurricane Florence just as the average remote volunteer, but I saw as soon as I joined the Cajun Navy how active things were. I saw how involved some of the other volunteers were, and I wanted to be part of that. I was trying to figure out a way to prove myself to what I thought of as the higher-ups," said Shane.

"I just knew them as the voices on Zello. I didn't really know anybody personally at the time, and we were all just getting to know each other. But the more active and vocal I was, I think I was able to solidify my place," Shane said.

Shane has always been serious about what we are doing, and he wanted to be a part of it. Even though he came in halfway through our Hurricane Florence efforts, he was able to help complete that mission.

"From the beginning, it felt good to know I contributed to what the Cajun Navy was doing," said Shane. "There was a lot of personal growth, because this was the first time I participated in the technology side of disaster relief. It really just grabbed ahold of me, because it was that instant communication. For example, I would see a Facebook post—this person needs flashlights, batteries, and some groceries. What can I do? What can I do to help with that? And even if I could personally deliver that, it just did not feel like it was enough."

Shane was not looking for a slap on the back, but he wanted to be a part of our mission. We never know what the next disaster or emergency will hold. We do things very quickly. We have to make knowledgeable and safe decisions and be able to execute those on the fly. No disaster is light, and you can have four hurricanes in a row with each one being completely different from the last one you dealt with.

You have to be prepared. You have to be open to doing something you may not be comfortable with or have not done before, even if it fails miserably. If you had not tried, you would not know what could have been. So you have to realize that there is a risk and that there is trial and error. You just do not know what it is you are going to come up against, but you have to be able to adjust and move forward, when and if something happens.

Hurricane Michael

We were barely wrapping up our deployment with Florence when Michael was making his way across the Atlantic. Very rapidly, this monster of a storm was churning in the Gulf of Mexico. Michael was the first Category 5 hurricane to strike the contiguous United States since Andrew in 1992. Michael turned into a hurricane very quickly. I think within two or three days of intensifying, it just slammed into the Panhandle of Florida. It was a lot like Hurricane Laura, in that its wind speed was very high. It completely decimated Mexico Beach.

We actually had someone on the phone with us while Michael slammed into her home in Florida. One of our dispatchers was speaking with a young lady who was in her teens or early twenties. As the hurricane made landfall, her windows blew out, and she was quite terrified. Then we suddenly lost contact, and it was several weeks before we were able to reach her again and confirm that she had survived and was OK.

Around this time, we noticed that some of the volunteers were being affected by all they had witnessed. We had gone straight into Hurricane Michael just weeks after Florence, and I could see that it was taking its toll on some volunteers. I know that witnessing traumatic events, or hearing survivors' stories of suffering and loss, can be very distressing. When volunteers live in the affected communities, the crisis may have impacted them and their families directly. They could also be reliving another trauma they have previously experienced.

When working in disaster relief, it is essential to remember that volunteers may have the same needs for assistance as those they are helping. You usually do not see it until after the storm has subsided, so to speak, and everything is calm. I always try to encourage volunteers to take breaks when they need them. They have to take care of their own wellbeing, live their lives, and spend time with their families. Otherwise, it is sure to cause problems.

One of the things we decided on to prepare for Michael was to have two team "leads" for the volunteers. We divided the area into two sections, one on each side of the highway headed up toward Atlanta, Georgia. Both teams staged in the different areas, waiting for the storm to hit. I think that was actually a really good idea, because Hurricane Michael would go right across 45 into Georgia, then into the Carolinas, then out into the Atlantic again.

As we prepared, we realized that we did not have the kind of lead time that Florence gave us. All we could do was watch what was happening with the hurricane as it approached and make a decision on what we should bring in.

We got our boats staged and ready to go. But to our surprise, there was very little flooding. Instead, the fast-moving storm brought powerful winds that decimated structures of all kinds. Debris and downed trees spread across many states. Power lines on the roads made them impassable. This was a big lesson for us. I realized that for fast-moving wind disasters such as this, we would need chainsaws and heavy equipment more than boats.

This required almost a whole different type of volunteer and way of thinking. We had all these guys who wanted to be out in their boats and rescuing people. When we spread the news that this was more of a wind event, many changed their attitudes to: *Oh well. I'm taking my boat and going home.* There is no rush or thrill from cutting up fallen trees. So many potential volunteers are simply not interested in joining that kind of relief effort.

In disaster response, you get different waves of volunteers. There are plenty who have the resources and the boats, and then when the rescues are done, they all go home. You find yourself looking for the next wave of volunteers, hoping they will not mind bringing their chainsaws and a team. You also need people to collect supplies and others to help distribute them. It is not always easy to get the right volunteers for the right task.

After Hurricane Michael passed, we got into our work gear, grabbed chainsaws, and started clearing roads of trees and debris. Next, we got busy coordinating volunteers. One such team from Wewahitchka, Florida began clearing roads in their community so that we could get to the more isolated places.

We discovered that it was very difficult to recruit volunteers in Florida. They have been hit by hurricanes so many times. But we ended up with quite a few boots on the ground for several weeks in Florida. We would have a bigger volunteer response later for Hurricane Laura, but the volunteers we had were dedicated.

Clearing roads and helping residents was what we did out there. Rain, shine, hot, cold—it did not matter. One team did this for almost thirty days. They were there helping Mr. Tony, one homeowner who was relieved and grateful to have our group out there. He said it was a major blessing to have us there, because otherwise he would not have been able to have the trees cut off of his house.

Mr. Tony was disabled. He had no homeowner's insurance, and he was denied funds by FEMA. Plus, removing one tree can take all day. As he said, if it had not been for us, there is no telling how long those trees would have stayed on his house. His roof was leaking, and sooner or later it would rain again. Then he would have even bigger problems. We were glad to be able to help him avoid those potential issues.

This particular team had been helping since Hurricane Michael hit. They drove in for four hours every single morning and then four hours back home every single night. They did that for several weeks, and they did not let up because they knew that people like Mr. Tony were counting on them.

Once our team finally got the trees off of his roof, they secured tarps on it. Our volunteers could see ominous clouds rolling in, so they worked as fast and as safely as they could. Mr. Tony would not have to worry about losing his home due to the mold that would grow in his house from the rain getting in. We knew we would have him all taken care of before the team left that day.

One big opportunity that we had was to work with the Coast Guard and other food suppliers to direct helicopters to the most isolated areas. In turn, we would direct volunteers to go unload those supplies once the helicopters arrived on site. After that, we could deliver those supplies right into the hands of people in the communities that needed them the most. Working with a helicopter operation was really a new experience for us.

Looking back, I would say that one of our biggest accomplishments there was securing and processing resources, both physical and informational. With multiple staging areas and helicopter drops, we were able to put so many supplies in the hands of people.

The Wewahitchka group was really dedicated to their town. They accomplished a lot of charitable work there, even planning a fall event for the children in that area. We called one of those volunteers the Fruit Lady. A photographer and mother, she had felt moved to help in that area after her kids came home from school saying they had new classmates whose families needed food.

The Fruit Lady would get donations of fresh fruit and load as much of it into her minivan as she could possibly pack. Then she would take it to the areas that needed it most. She traveled to places where people had completely lost their homes. Many were living in tents out in a field. The Fruit Lady made multiple trips, and the people of Florida were grateful for her.

It is great when you have one volunteer who says, "I could start a donation drive," and another who could drive supplies out to the community. Volunteerism is an amazing thing when it can be utilized properly. When everything is aligned, volunteers can efficiently help those in need, at exactly the right moment.

Michael was the strongest storm ever to strike the Florida Panhandle. It hit very fast, and it was shocking to see how it just slammed into the coast. Initially, it was recorded as four or five miles shy of a Category 5. The next year, it was upgraded to Category 5. It is interesting how people who were not directly affected have forgotten about Hurricane Michael by now and don't talk about it. But I am quite sure that many who live there are still recovering from it.

Chapter 5

More Disasters

A lot happened in a short period of time. On the heels of Florence and Michael, we became engaged in the California wildfires; flooding events in South Dakota, Nebraska, Tennessee, and Mississippi; and tornado-ravaged areas in and around Dayton, Ohio. During that time span, we were able to show communities how to use technology to check on homes, look for pets, and organize search parties for missing people. We also demonstrated how to use technology to efficiently place people in shelters or temporary housing and move supplies when and where they were needed most.

I knew that someone had to come in and tell these stories, to keep the rest of the world from forgetting.

During the 2018 wildfires in California, including the Paradise fire, we began posting accounts on our Facebook page, and we streamed the victims' stories on Facebook Live. We also shared those videos on CrowdRelief. In addition, we gave accounts from our volunteers on location.

One such search-and-rescue volunteer traveled around and tried to help in so many ways. He came with his two rescue dogs from Michigan to California. When he reached his destination of Oroville, California, he had traveled 2,459 miles in two and a half days. We also partnered with a woman who was a California resident and a photographer.

During that time, we developed a remote and ground team of about twenty people who had been working well together for a couple of years. They were just individual volunteers who began to band together, and many of them were able to take on leadership roles within our organization.

I think it is important to talk not just about the people who join our cause but also those who decide to drop out. There is no way around the fact that volunteers come and go. This work can drain all of your energy; that is the nature of it. You can give a lot of yourself in this field, and it is difficult to try to balance what you're doing with family, jobs, and a lot of things. You get so busy that sometimes you put the people you care about on the back burner.

Shane explained it this way.

"With every disaster, it is relief and recovery that is on the forefront. My wife always says, especially during Michael, that she was a disaster widow for several weeks. If I was not on the phone, I was on Zello or Facebook—from the time I got up until the wee hours of the morning. And you know, we had long enough to maybe sit down and have a meal together, and then thirty minutes later I was back at it. It takes a toll, not only on the people who are doing it, but on the people in the background who are supporting them as well."

I cannot stress enough the importance of being able to do what you can do—and then going back to your life. It is imperative that you not make disasters your number-one focus, because they really are a drain. Michael was a big learning experience for us as a team. Looking back, we saw how crucial it is that we responders take care of our own mental and physical welfare.

We have to have an understanding that we are volunteers, and we have families and jobs and lives. I think that was the big takeaway from Michael. It was for me, anyway. We want our volunteers to consider their own welfare and not get burned out.

Everyone recovering from a disaster is still dealing with trauma. We can do our part by helping. But there are always things we just cannot fix. I would say that probably 98 percent of the time, we never see the people we are helping. We may never know their names or meet them in person, but we have to remind ourselves that we still made a difference in their lives.

Some days, though, we are able to touch lives on a personal level, and we will remember those names forever.

Tropical Storm Imelda

Then there was Tropical Storm Imelda. She caused devastating and record-breaking floods in southeast Texas. In September 2019, Imelda rapidly developed into a tropical storm before moving ashore near Freeport. She weakened after making landfall but continued bringing flooding rain to Texas and Louisiana for days.

Imelda's flooding hit in the early morning hours, and 911 emergency lines were down. That's when requests for rescues and other assistance poured in to the Cajun Navy Ground Force. We coordinated volunteer efforts and delivered help and supplies to those in need.

I remember that nobody really anticipated what would happen. I still have the text messages that started coming in early in the morning. My phone was blowing up at 5:00 A.M. People were afraid because they woke up to flooding homes, and they had no idea what to do.

Our volunteers jumped into action. Our social-media team was flooded with messages on Facebook, from people needing to be rescued, people looking for family members, and people just asking questions. We do not always have the answers right away, but we are always able to walk the survivors through the process, step by step by step. They know we are there and will not leave them, whatever that means for their particular situation.

Sometimes it means staying on the phone with someone during a storm to let them know they are not alone. Other times it means doing a wellness check on a loved one with whom they cannot make contact. It can be as simple as answering a Facebook question about where to find water or which roads are passable. On the ground, our teams can provide an even more personal touch. For someone who has just lost everything, a stranger offering them a cup of coffee and a hug might be the highlight of their day.

The text message I woke up to at 5:00 A.M. looked like this. There was an address, along with the words, "Elderly trapped in apartment. Can't walk. Please help." That was the first. People started calling me right after that, and it did not stop all day. It was a continuous whirlwind of calls, texts, and me responding as quickly as I possibly could.

These were coming from numbers I did not even know and from different area codes. At 5:24 A.M., I read this message: "There was an all call sent out about an hour ago for Cherokee County in Texas. They're asking for evacuation by boat." Another message, still before 6:00 A.M., read, "Please help with rescue. 92-year-old, elderly, 75-year-old, 70-year-old, and a 65-year-old, flooded."

We were able to get rolling with rescues immediately, and we didn't even have to send our own team to the scene. We used technology to connect with people there on the ground. And since we had already been there for Harvey, it was not too hard to start putting the word out that we needed rescue boaters right away. Within an hour, we had people in boats going out and doing rescues.

We just got in and started helping right away. The model of other groups is to load up their boats, meet somewhere in their city, and all drive over to the disaster together. That takes a lot of time, and when you need to be rescued, you need it now. I remember thinking, *Oh wow . . . wait. . . . These other groups did not get there until like seven o'clock that night, whereas we had started about twelve hours earlier.*

How did we do that? We were already rolling on rescues because we sourced everything locally. The rescuers we can engage live in the very areas being affected. We have our groups of volunteers already staged. Some of the other groups were waiting for people to get home from work, pack up their boats, and get their teams together before they could come in.

I realized that what we do is very unique. We can respond much more quickly. This tropical storm really exposed that.

The other storm we responded to that year was Hurricane Barry. It was just a Category 1, but its winds did a lot of damage along the Gulf Coast. I remember Barry because, fittingly enough, at the time I was co-hosting the ten-part television show *Mutant Weather*, about climate change.

Chapter 6

Being a Cajun Navy Ground Force Volunteer

In 2017, I changed the name of our foundation to Cajun Navy Foundation (CNF). Unlike the other Cajun Navy groups, who limit their scope to direct action on the ground, CNF is an action-oriented think tank consisting of a diverse team of technology, social-media, disaster-relief, and rescue professionals. As a 501(c)(3) charity, we seek to empower communities across the country to use technology and social media to take action in the midst and aftermath of a local disaster. We are working together to understand how to respond quickly during the chaos of disaster, when first responders and authorities may be overwhelmed. As for the crisis that follows the event, we have found that our greatest opportunities lie in involving citizens in helping with the enormous rebuilding and recovery efforts.

As we continue to learn from experience and adapt to ever-evolving technology, we recognize that our volunteers are our greatest assets. With their extensive and diverse backgrounds, skill sets, and strengths, we strive to maximize our collective impact by engaging volunteers where they are most needed. In our organization, people bring their talents to the table and use them in ways that complement one another. The diversity of experience, backgrounds, and personalities—combined with the love for helping others that we have in common—is the perfect recipe for a strong team.

None of our volunteers became a part of our mission by chance. Each team member has a gift to share and a need to be a part of something much bigger than themselves. Every one of them has a story to tell.

Michelle Szinavel's Story

I met Rob online because we were both outdoor enthusiasts. Rob knew that I had worked for NASDAQ for the two previous years and that I had a computer and technical background. During the Louisiana flood of 2016, he contacted me and asked if I could start posting information on a new Facebook group designed to help. I started off posting weather reports, street flooding, and mostly that kind of information.

At that time, I had never really volunteered for anything. I had participated in walks and those kinds of events, but I had never volunteered at a soup kitchen, for example. I have helped with various causes such as donating money for cancer, United Way, Shriners, St. Jude, and veterans' causes. Anyway, I agreed to help with the postings and that was the end of it, so I thought.

Then Hurricane Harvey was coming, and Rob asked again if I could take care of social media for him. *Wow!* I think I spoke to more than eight hundred people in just the inbox. I spoke to boaters, people who needed rescue, people looking for people, and people who wanted to dispatch. There were *so many people.* And I managed to push many of them to our Twitter, Instagram, our Facebook group, and Zello to drive more engagement.

I had no idea it would be such an incredible experience . . . heartbreaking and scary, but also emotional because of the outpouring of people wanting to help. I think I slept two hours during that entire time. I did not want to miss anyone who needed help. Some people just wanted to talk because they were scared.

Like I said earlier, I never really volunteered. Before any of this, I had become ill. I could not work and I became very depressed. I stayed in bed and slept, and that sucked. I was suffering and in pain. Around the same time, my dad passed away and that was devastating to me. We were always very close, and even now after all these years—just writing about it, I want to cry.

I originally thought I was doing Rob a favor by helping out, but really it was the other way around. Now I had a purpose. And even though I physically felt terrible, I got out of bed because I had to take care of social media. After the storms were done and most of the volunteers got back to their lives, I continued to post information on the pages and groups. I posted anything that I thought citizens might need to know, like deadlines for services, etc., even information about other resources, such as when a food pantry needed donations.

Other storms came—Irma, Maria, Florence, Michael, Laura, and others. So each time, I volunteered. Over the years, I have seen so much devastation, but I have also seen how great people can be to each other. Religion, politics, ethnicity? None of that mattered. It is a wonderful thing to see, just people helping people.

I have seen people who have lost their homes, and yet they want to help others. I admire them so much, and it is humbling. It breaks my heart when I see these disasters—the lives lost, the homes destroyed, families having to leave their communities and sometimes each other to live with other family members. Many of the survivors often feel embarrassed and are afraid to ask for help.

It gives me hope, knowing that no matter how bad things are, there is someone who will drop everything to help. I love seeing people reaching out to each other and communities banding together. The hard part is when the cameras go away. We have to keep people engaged and coming in to volunteer on the ground when the time comes to rebuild. That is what Cajun Navy Ground Force (CNGF, formerly Cajun Navy Foundation) and CrowdRelief are all about. We keep reminding people that there is still a need. I know a lot of people want to get in their boats and come rescue, and we need that, but we need them to come afterward, too.

Now I have transitioned to working in the background. I try to give our volunteers the tools that they need to do their part and help those in need. Volunteering has been one of the best things I have ever experienced, and I recommend that everyone do it—even if it is just sharing a post about food being cooked for victims or ground volunteers. I am thankful for the friends I have made. I am thankful for the wonderful volunteers who work so tirelessly. I am more thankful that I have been able to volunteer with the Cajun Navy, and for what it has done for me, than I can express.

AJ Martin's Story

What do you do when you have multiple friends asking if the organization that you have been a part of is going to help out during another type of natural disaster that is not a hurricane?

Most of my friends know that since I got hurt a few years ago, I have been putting my skills learned over twenty-five years of being a paramedic to use helping where I can. When Hurricane Laura came to see us, I signed up to work alongside the Cajun Navy. After dealing with one of the most active storm seasons on record, I, like everyone else, took a break to recharge and regroup for the upcoming season.

Little did we know that in February 2021, we would face a different type of storm. It was an ice storm. Having lived in southeast Texas my whole life, I know we have had some interesting winter weather; but in that time, I had never ever seen or heard of what we dealt with that year. Every county in Texas was affected by it.

We had snow on the beaches in Galveston and Corpus Christi. In some places, it looked like the Great Lakes Area. This is Texas. We do not get that type of weather. So after getting more texts, calls, and messages asking if the Cajun Navy was going to have a response here in my hometown of Beaumont, I did the only thing I could think of: I called Rob.

I explained the situation here in town and asked if we could do anything. We have a population of around 114,000 people in Beaumont alone. If you add in the rest of the Golden Triangle, not to mention Hardin County, we have close to 350,000 in three counties. Rob told me if I could find a place to set up, to go for it. So I called my city councilman, who is also a good friend, Mike Getz, and asked about a place for us to stage here in town.

Mike informed me that he was just talking to another friend of mine about just that. I called Rob back, and then got Mike on the phone with us so we could figure out the best options for what we wanted to do. Our entire area was without an active water supply from the storm. Mike made some calls and we initially were going to use Ford Park for our staging area.

I called Charles Teel and asked him if he could come help out with ground ops, and we started working. Within six hours of that first phone call, we had a plan in place to get started. This was on Saturday. Unfortunately, the plans fell through with Ford Park due to unforeseen circumstances. Charles called his pastor at St. Mark's and asked if we could use the church instead. They were more than happy to help, and all those plans shifted to his church downtown.

Having lived and worked in Beaumont all my life, I started reaching out to everyone that I felt could help. Charles did the same, and our plans really started moving. Rob sent help from our Lake Charles operation that was still ongoing to back us up. With the help of Sam's Club, H-E-B Grocery, Market Basket supermarkets, and Zummo Meat Company, we got water and food to pass out for our folks here at home.

From Sunday to Wednesday, we handed out 6,000 cases of water. We cooked between 300 and 400 hamburgers and link sausages for our community. We had local volunteers from all walks of life who just wanted to be a part of what we were doing. It was a total team effort, from the donations we received to the time given. We had students from my wife's high school, Beaumont United, who came out and helped all four days.

I had put a call out to the activities directors for both of our main high schools, telling them if they had kids needing service hours I would be happy to sign off on them if they came out to help. With all the turmoil going on in our country today, it was amazing to watch a community come together for a common goal . . . just helping their neighbors.

Having that support made my job as Team Lead that much easier. I was asked quite a few times, during and after: how did we get it all done? My response was always the same. We just do what is right, and then it works

Thinking back on it now, seven Cajun Navy Ground Force personnel were here. The rest were just our hometown neighbors. What we did made a difference in so many lives. That makes all of what we do mean something. I'm just glad to be a small part in a bigger endeavor.

As we were wrapping up our Beaumont op, Rob asked me if I would go and help out in Denton, Texas, which is in the Dallas-Fort Worth area. So Thursday morning, I got on a flight to DFW from Beaumont to help out another community that was hit just as hard, if not harder, than we were. I spent three days in the Denton area, helping Operation Airdrop and a local community group get food and supplies to 5,800 families.

This was just another way that we as the Cajun Navy Ground Force made a difference. We do not do what we do for the accolades or fanfare. We are just people helping others when they need it the most.

Shane Callcut's Story

My first experience with disaster relief was with Hurricane Katrina, when I volunteered to go down from Arkansas and help with cleanup and hand out supplies. It is an experience I will never forget: the sights, sounds, and smells. You cannot forget it. Then several disasters later, I began helping in the background. In 2011, I became a disaster survivor myself when we were flooded out by the Mississippi River and had nothing but the clothes on our backs.

We went to work, and we came home to nothing. After that, following the Joplin, Missouri tornado, I started volunteering more locally in Arkansas. It has been an amazing experience ever since. This is my calling—this is what I do.

I first came on board with Cajun Navy Ground Force during Hurricane Florence, and it carried over into the next disaster, Michael. I became a moderator on the Cajun Navy Zello channel, and eventually I took the lead in Zello communications. As a moderator on Zello, I field questions and concerns while keeping the room free of spam and open to everyone in need of help. I try to offer a calm voice, and I strive to give direction to those seeking assistance.

During the days following Hurricane Michael, I stayed very busy on Zello. On one particular day, I worked twelve-plus hours. It is always a bit chaotic, with so many volunteers needing vetting, others bringing supplies, and many coming to volunteer as boots on the ground. In addition, there is administrative work to be done. My position on Zello is a challenge, but I would not have it any other way.

I firmly believe that the correct response to someone sharing a problem is not: "Everything's going to be OK." The correct response is: "I'm sorry. What can I do to help?"

Several thousand volunteers signed up to serve with Cajun Navy Ground Force in the two months following Hurricanes Florence and Michael. That speaks to why we are one of the best organizations out there when it comes to disaster relief. We are everyday citizens saving lives and providing the relief resources necessary for those affected. From disaster to rebuilding, we are there. We will not stand down.

Lori Kirkpatrick's Story

I was at my home in the small coastal town of Hampstead, North Carolina when Hurricane Florence struck. My house had sustained some roof and siding damage, but it seemed inconsequential as I looked around at my neighbors. Two houses down from me on lower ground, flooding from the torrential rain had reached the floor of the home. I watched my neighbor wade through the water as he tried to salvage what he could, carrying armloads of family treasures to higher ground.

The destruction was much worse on the western side of the county. Many homes had been flooded, and the residents had watched their lives wash away. As the days passed, I heard countless stories of all that had been lost. My heart broke for them. I wanted to do something to help, but what?

Time stood still for the eleven days I spent without power. My days consisted of cooking makeshift meals on a single-burner propane stove, searching for places that were giving away ice, and bathing with gallon jugs of water that I had picked up in a supply line at a Lowe's Home Improvement parking lot. It was September, but the heat and humidity were suffocating. However, as bad as it seemed, these were mere inconveniences compared to people who would go much, much longer without the luxuries of electricity, hot meals, air conditioning, or even a roof over their heads.

Everything in coastal North Carolina was shut down. Even after the stores began to open back up, it did not matter because the shelves were empty. I teach at a community college, and classes were canceled for a month after Florence. I was also writing for a local newspaper, so that was my only means of income during that time. One thing was certain: there was certainly no shortage of stories to write.

It was just a matter of getting to the people to hear their stories. Yes, I could find potential topics in my Facebook newsfeed, and I could reach out by calling or emailing others I heard about. But it was a tough time, and I did not want to bother people when they were suffering such loss and trying to recover from this terrible storm. So I decided that I would try to focus on stories of people helping people.

I happened to hear on the radio that the Cajun Navy was coming to our area. Curious, I looked them up on Facebook. I came across a Facebook Live video and decided to watch to learn more about them. It was Rob asking for volunteers. I went to their Facebook page and sent a message. I explained that I write for a local newspaper, and I wanted to write an article about them coming to Pender County (where I lived).

I received a response from one of the volunteers right away, and we set up a time for me to interview Rob. After I wrote the article and sent a copy to Rob, he soon called to ask me if I would be interested in writing blogs for the Cajun Navy. At this point, I had been sitting home in the aftermath of Florence, and I was still without power. I thought, *Why not?* I knew I would have to get creative to find a place with Wi-Fi where I could work. But I thought maybe this was how I could help—getting information out to the people who needed it.

First, Rob added me to all of the Cajun Navy Facebook groups and chats, and I added the Zello app to my phone. I spent some time just listening to everything that was going on around me. The dispatchers, the social-media team, Zello communications, mapping, resources—they were using any technology you can imagine to assist with rescues, supply distribution, and just helping people with any needs that arose.

It was easier to get involved when I finally got electricity and Wi-Fi at my house. Now I would not have to search for a place where I could write. I listened intently to all that was happening, and when I heard something interesting, I would just reach out to the volunteers who were involved. I would interview them or send them questions to answer, and then I would use the information I had gathered to write blogs to post on the Cajun Navy's website. For a while, I was posting several blogs a day, and they were a mix of stories of rescues, survivors, and volunteers; all calls for volunteers; and requests for supplies and volunteers. I wrote about anything that stood out to me.

We quickly transitioned from Hurricane Florence to Hurricane Michael relief efforts, and I continued writing blogs. We had teams cutting trees and tarping homes, supply distribution, and even helicopter supply drops. There was never a shortage of topics to write about. I continued helping during the California wildfires, Tropical Storm Imelda, Hurricane Laura, and other events. I gradually transitioned from blog writing to assisting with social-media content, posting on social media, answering rescue requests and questions that come in, public relations, communication, and writing policies and procedures.

As a Cajun Navy volunteer, I have witnessed the importance of telling the stories of survivors. I have seen how easily the people who were only minimally affected by a storm can forget how much their neighbors still need their help. The effects linger for months and even years. If telling their stories brings their needs to light, or makes a difference for just one family, it is worth it.

I will admit, telling survivor stories can be an emotional task. There is often a sense of sadness involved. But the sadness could never outweigh the hope and healing that I have seen the Cajun Navy bring to the people who need it and when they need it most.

A Zello Conversation

In a conversation on the CrowdRelief Zello channel, one Cajun Navy Ground Force volunteer named Brian said, "To do what we do, it is not easy. It takes a lot out of you physically, emotionally, and financially. It's like the links of a chain and sprocket. It takes everybody to be able to turn and be able to work. Some of this stuff, you don't get over when you go home. I mean, you still see it, hear it, the smells, but it's worth it in the end."

One of our dispatchers named Sandy responded, "That is why I have always done it. . . . It is worth it in the end. I've been a helper since I was seventeen years old, and I did my first disaster in 1994. I would have to sit down and think about how many I have done since then that I have assisted with in some way. I think with the Cajun Navy Ground Force, and with CrowdRelief, I have found my home. This is where I am going to be for a long time—with you guys. I look forward to working with you guys because we are such a well-put-together team at this point that it is just amazing."

Another Zello Conversation

Cajun Navy Ground Force's citizen volunteers know firsthand that no act of kindness is ever too small. One conversation on the group's Zello channel demonstrated that hope can blossom from the slightest of thoughtful gestures. What seems minor at the time can mean the world to a family member who has lost contact with a loved one during and following a disaster.

During the Zello conversation, some of the citizen volunteers were discussing the occurrences of the day. One of them, along with other boots on the ground, had taken the time to walk house to house collecting phone numbers of family members. Later, once she had good "calling out" mobile service again, she reached out to someone's son out of state. She told him that his mother was safe. The woman's son had not known until that moment that she was even still alive. He cried, relieved by the news. He was more than thankful for the act of kindness, and it certainly brightened the volunteer's day.

A CNF dispatcher, touched by the story, responded.

"I am going to cry," she began. "I wish that everybody would do that, because that is the scariest thing. There are so many people . . . they just need to know that their people are OK—their friends, their family. So what you did is beyond amazing. You are an angel.

Another volunteer added, "Sometimes in life, we get busy and caught up in everyday life, and just the little things like that—checking on our neighbors, the elderly, and things like that—just going the extra mile means so much, you know? There are people out there that just need that, and something like that can go a long, long way."

The conversation concluded with a prayer by another volunteer who prayed on Zello every day. He began with thankfulness for the good news. Then he prayed for help for CNF volunteers, moment by moment and minute by minute; for provision, nourishment, and sustenance; and finally, for guidance to get the CNF volunteers to the people who need their help.

Robin Hall's Story

I came to Lake Charles knowing I was never going to be Superman in a boat. I did, however, come here believing I could make a difference on a different level. I originally was drawn here by a video of a ninety-two-year-old woman living in her car six months after Hurricane Laura. I mistakenly believed she was a rare case.

The first job I did in Lake Charles was helping a woman move some damaged furniture to the road, clearing debris, and removing what was left of her fence. That job was the one that I will never forget. It was humbling. It opened my eyes, my mind, and my heart to the deep suffering these people were experiencing.

She and I spent a fair amount of time talking. She told me she could not talk to her family, friends, and neighbors because it was the same story so many of them had lived. She walked me through her house with a somberness I can't forget. She told me, "You never really know what you have to lose, until you lose it all. After the hurricane, I came back. My roof was in my yard, and it was a mess. My roof had giant holes, there were inches of water in my home, rain running down my walls . . . and I thought, *Where do I begin?*" She told me she began in her yard, because it was not as heartbreaking as picking up the memories floating in her home.

My entire life I have seen a chair as being a functional piece of furniture you sit in to rest your body. She gave me a different perspective. The chair we carried to the road was not just a chair. It was where she had sat in times of happiness and in times of sorrow. It was where she held her grandchild for the first time and where she sat every Christmas as the family gathered to open gifts. It was one more thing that held and triggered her memories, and it was just one more loss she had to suffer.

The perspective she gave me carried through the six months I was in Lake Charles. It helped me understand the reactions and gratitude we received even over the simple things. When we delivered an air conditioner to a mother with a young child not dealing well with the heat, it was more than just a way to keep cool. It was a good night's sleep for an exhausted parent. When we delivered food and water to a mother of five, it was not just a meal. It was removing the stress from a mother who was worried about her kids' next meal. Even something as simple as reflectors at the end of a driveway were more than just ten dollars' worth of plastic. It was another step in helping the woman feel some of the safety she had pre-hurricane.

The strength, the faith, the hearts of the people in Southwest Louisiana will forever be imprinted on my soul. The lessons I learned in six months will continue to be invaluable to me throughout the rest of my life.

Camille Domingue's Story

The day Rob left in preparation for Hurricane Laura, everyone was tense, as the storm appeared to be heading for my hometown, Lafayette. At the last minute, Laura changed course and headed toward Port Arthur, Texas, then Lake Charles. Rob and I had been dating about seven months by that time, and I was well aware of his part in the Cajun Navy and all of the disaster efforts of the storms before me. But nothing could have prepared me for what was to come.

Rob's phone was blowing up; he had four calls going all at the same time. We were driving through the city of Lafayette gathering the things he would take with him, along with every other person preparing for the storm to come. The grocery-store shelves were empty, there were long lines for gas, and to top it off there was a protest happening through the city at the same time. It was a peaceful march for Trayford Pellerin, a young Black man killed by local police. My head was swimming trying to process everything. Rob looked over at me and asked, "Are you ready for all of this?"

I had no idea what would unfold in the ten months to follow.

As Laura battered the coast of Louisiana, Rob and I were able to maintain contact until the storm reached Lake Charles. He was sending photos and videos and even managed a few calls, then nothing . . . radio silence. Then, the winds died down and the sun came up, revealing Laura's destruction. Luckily, Lafayette was spared, but Lake Charles and the surrounding communities would be changed forever.

The first call came in—Rob was safe and scouting the city with his first volunteers. He described the scene and it sounded really grim. I have never been to war, or spent any time in a war zone, but the images that were coming through my phone took my breath away. I am named after a hurricane: Hurricane Camille. I've heard about its destruction all my life, but now Hurricane Laura would be the name on people's lips.

A day later, Rob called again. He and his volunteers had found a place to stage. They were standing on asphalt, baking in the sun and in danger of dehydration. They needed supplies to distribute, but nothing was available to them: no food, water, or anything else. Everything for miles around had been wiped out by the storm. Rob asked if I could bring things from Lafayette. I made calls to friends and local grocery stores and asked for their help. By noon, my car and my girlfriend's truck were loaded down with donations and headed for Lake Charles. I had packed a small bag "just in case." I'll never forget what I saw driving into that beaten city and onto the scene that would become the new reality of our lives for the months to come.

Chaos, destruction, fear, and sheer adrenaline swirled around me. Power lines and glass, metal, and crumbled bricks were thrown everywhere. Massive oak trees had been plucked from the ground. Water covered structures, and where there was dry ground, dogs ran loose with their leashes still attached to their necks. Hot, sweaty, weary people wandered around with no place to go. It resembled a war zone, and now I know firsthand what that is like.

Then, I saw Rob. Without question, I knew I'd be staying. He hadn't slept a full night in a couple of days. He was operating at full throttle—adrenaline had completely taken over. His feet and legs were sunburned, he was covered in scratches, his eyes had deep dark circles under them, and he was drenched in sweat. He smiled at me and thanked me and my friends for coming and helping. As quickly as he appeared, he disappeared, pulled in yet another direction.

Just before he left, he asked if I was OK. I said I wasn't sure what to do or where I was needed the most. My friends were gone and I knew no one there other than Rob. There was no time for introductions. He looked at me and said, "Just jump in." And in a flash, he was gone. I had never volunteered during a disaster before. I was not accustomed to the heat, the sights, the smells, the people coming from everywhere. But I did what he asked and jumped in with both feet.

That was only the beginning. Little did I know that this mission would not end anytime soon—no one did.

There have been so many faces, stories, and more disasters since then. The rate at which the organization grew was head spinning. Volunteers and support continued to flow in. The outreach through Facebook continued to feed the efforts of our team and help so many people in need. That's a beautiful thing, right? Yes, but with that exposure comes harsh criticism and judgment.

We were still in the throes of a pandemic, a volatile presidential election, and an unprecedented season of natural disasters. People were testy. You have to accept the thorns with the rose.

Rob has shared his vision with me so many times: the sacrifices, the trials, the triumphs. Not many people know what it is like behind the scenes. Working 24/7 month after month doesn't come without bumps and bruises. Chaos becomes your life. It takes great mental strength to persevere and push through.

Everyone at some point is stretched to their limit. It takes a toll on your family, your career, your finances, your mental health, and especially your relationships. It's only with a shared vision and mission, and love and support, that people or an organization can see their way through.

People and volunteers along the way become family and lifetime friends. There is also heartache along the way—goodbyes you never imagined you'd have to say. For better or for worse, you are now forever woven into the story of another person's life. You smile when you remember the face of the first person you helped, yet you are haunted by the frailty of the human condition.

I have witnessed so much good—the kindness of people who genuinely want to help. They give from their hearts. You show up to help someone in need, and they end up helping you. Nothing else in the world matters during a disaster. Disaster becomes your world. It is all about helping that person in front of you any way you can, even if all you can give is a smile.

Mr. Johnny was the very first person I helped face to face and really connected with. He drove an old 1950s Chevrolet truck just like my dad's. He was about seventy-two years old and had the sweetest smile. Mr. Johnny had no children or family around. He desperately needed a tarp on his roof.

I met him in a parking lot behind a building where we were staged. It was lunchtime, so I invited him into the building, out of the heat, since we had a generator running air conditioning in there. We fixed Mr. Johnny some lunch, and I got him bags of supplies for later. We filled out a request for help with dispatch, and he was on his way.

Three weeks later, I walked out of the building and Mr. Johnny was waiting for me. He had been looking for me for a few days. I was so happy to see him! He had gone to all that trouble to thank me. He told me that he would never forget me and that his family was praying for me every day by name. I was in tears. Who helped whom?

What I have learned about life and human nature through this experience is that people are inherently good, not everyone shows up for the right reasons, disaster burnout is real, sometimes the good suffer for the bad, even the smallest act of kindness can make all the difference in someone's life, and love endures.

Chapter 7

The Role of Technology

Technology is how I got involved in the disaster field. It is my professional background. The Louisiana flooding was not the first time I did anything related to technology and disasters. In fact, I had the opportunity to build a technology platform for Hurricane Katrina in 2005. There were even several studies done on it.

Hurricane Katrina made landfall on the coast of Louisiana on August 29, 2005. It approached as a strong Category 5 storm, and it hit land as a Category 3, with winds reaching speeds as high as 125 miles per hour. Due to the destruction and loss of life that Katrina caused, the storm is considered one of the worst in our country's history. About 1,200 deaths in Louisiana have been directly connected to the hurricane. It was also the costliest storm up to that point, causing $125 billion in property damage.

Hurricane Katrina brought to light a series of deep-rooted problems in disaster response. There were controversies over the federal government's response, difficulties with search-and-rescue efforts, and a serious lack of preparedness for the storm. Fifty-three of the city's levees failed during the hurricane, causing devastating flooding and damage in the low-lying city. Many victims of Katrina were low income and African American, and those who lost their homes faced years of hardship.

After Hurricane Katrina struck, quite a lot of evacuees were sent to shelters away from New Orleans. During this process, people were just loaded onto buses and driven outside of the danger zone. At the time, I lived in Shreveport. Many of those survivors were sent to a place up there known as Hirsch Coliseum, and I went to volunteer.

I had a friend who was running that shelter. I happened to be developing a software platform for him. His name is Romy Cucjen, and he was a baseball coach. At that time, he had invented an incredible throwing machine that was far superior to what had been in use. The machine would not only throw like a typical pitch, but it would also throw from home plate and simulate someone hitting a fly ball or a ground ball, for example.

I wrote the software user interface for Romy's machine. So when I found out he was running the shelter, I offered to come and work with him. I knew there would be much to do, and I was sure he could use some extra hands. I arrived and began just helping in any way I could. I noticed that they had a bank of computers set up, so I walked over to check it out. I saw that people were using this area to try to locate family members who had been missing since the storm.

Social media was in its infancy in 2005. Really the best the survivors could do for communication was just check their emails on the computers. I kept watching the people, and eventually I offered to help them find their family members. I accomplished this by researching various shelters online. As I checked to see if they listed the people sheltering there, word was spreading about what I was doing.

A lot of survivors started coming to me and requesting help in finding their families. I ended up asking people I knew who were working from home to do research, as well. I saw an opportunity to use my software-development skills to build a system for locating missing loved ones. So I built it right there at the Hirsch. I created a website to track the searches using the ASP programming language, Notepad, and an Access database. Once complete, I uploaded the site to my webserver and started making entries. Then I asked friends at home to log in and try to locate these missing people.

That is how it took off. I was just a guy with a talent for

writing software, so I decided next to devise a ticket system. A survivor could walk up to us at a computer at the shelter and ask for help finding a lost family member. The person at the computer would enter the information into the system, and then we could create a ticket number. The remote researchers would locate the other shelters and call them to ask about the missing family member. These shelters were spread all across the southern region, from Dallas to Florida.

They also sent some survivors up toward Fort Smith and Little Rock, so I started having other volunteers look at those. We would give the person in the shelter their ticket number, and then they could come back later in the day or the next day and see if anybody had found new information about their family. That is how it worked—volunteers sitting at home doing research, trying to locate people's lost relatives. That was really the first time I ever used technology in a disaster.

Several universities conducted a study about my method for finding missing family members. My next use of technology to help in a disaster was when I was on Facebook during the 2016 Louisiana flooding.

At that time, I already had an office in Baton Rouge, so it made sense for me to operate from there. I decided to call in various friends and acquaintances that I knew had worked in technology. Michelle Szinavel was one of those people I asked to help. She is the original volunteer. Michelle was a friend of mine before any of the disaster work, since we had been collaborating on some other interesting technology projects.

My friendship with Michelle started when we connected online as outdoor enthusiasts. Later, I was rewriting old newspaper articles and organizing them into a platform. I had decided to rewrite accounts of historic undocumented creatures because the old articles had not been scanned very well and were difficult to read. I knew that making them legible meant that they would be searchable. Michelle helped me with the rewriting. We still have that database with all of those pieces of writing in it, and I believe she rewrote about two hundred really fascinating articles.

In 2017, Hurricane Harvey took our attention. Like me, Michelle had just fallen into the disaster world, and responding was now natural for her. She started setting up Google forms and spreadsheets for the Cajun Navy Ground Force.

She also became the go-to person for answering questions and pointing new volunteers in the right direction whenever they needed help. Before long, she had taken on the role of being the other person (along with myself) who basically holds the keys to the kingdom. She keeps up with all of the passwords and documents, among other responsibilities.

I had to acknowledge an essential truth—I needed help with running the organization. I have never thought that I could do it all myself. I know I cannot, and I realize that I have to allow other people to take on responsibilities and to be confident that they will keep operations moving in a positive direction.

What kept us together as volunteers is technology. Without it, there was absolutely no way for us to connect as a team and be able to expand and help as many people as we helped. We have had volunteers from all over. We have been able to assist people across the country and even some in other countries.

Everything we have accomplished could only be possible with the use of technology. It has helped us help others in a variety of ways. First, we can communicate with Zello and Facebook Messenger. We use Facebook groups to communicate among ourselves and with the public. For at least one hurricane season, we also used Microsoft Teams. This enabled us to save all of our documents within that platform and share them with one another as needed.

Another notable aspect of the Cajun Navy Ground Force's use of technology is the tracking of data. We operate as a dispatch system. We create tickets for rescue and relief, and then dispatchers take those tickets and find volunteers on the ground. They do that using the technology of a GPS app. We direct the volunteers on the ground to go out and perform the rescues. The volunteers, or boots on the ground, are then able to provide insights during the rescues that will help us make decisions about subsequent efforts in the area.

Additionally, we train volunteers specifically to do background vetting of other volunteers as they come in. We have found these checks to be a necessary part of our volunteer onboarding process. It is important to understand that our volunteers may encounter individuals in distress, as well as those separated from family. Conducting a background check before taking on a disaster-response volunteer serves as a safeguard to ensure that our volunteers will not pose a risk to individuals in need of real and timely assistance.

We have been fortunate to have this vetting service donated to us by an organization named InfoMart. InfoMart is a fast-growing global technology company, established in 1989 as a US screening and data provider. As an added measure, we check the potential volunteer's Facebook page to make sure they are a good fit for our organization and will align with our mission. We also had a company called Pocketstop donate their service. They have provided an SMS messaging app for the Cajun Navy Ground Force to use.

Technology is embedded into the very fabric of everything we do as a team. For example, we ask our volunteers, who are working from all over the country, to sign electronic nondisclosure agreements. We use these to protect sensitive information about survivors we have assisted.

We also use other social media at times, as we push out information during a disaster. We have used Twitter, but I have to admit that we have not used it to its full potential. In general, we have found that Facebook is where the general population is. That is where people typically search for information or request help.

However, I do realize that there are a lot of Twitter users. During Hurricane Harvey, I had gone on Twitter and started posting for people to hop on our Zello channels. That proved to be quite helpful, and we ended up with a lot of volunteers from Twitter who came over to Facebook and Zello to join us.

The more I think about it, I would actually like to start utilizing that again and building up a base. I know that Twitter has the potential for great numbers of informational followers, as well as people we can depend on with reliable information that we can retweet. But as far as our main focus of getting information out there, we have traditionally relied heavily on Facebook and on Zello. They allow us to pull volunteers from across the country. The only potential challenge is that they have to know how to get on Zello and speak with us using the app.

One thing that we are working on and would like to be able to do more consistently is to take content and make sure it gets pushed out into all of the platforms, including Twitter. In fact, we are currently working on a campaign to drive volunteers. We plan to do that by targeting ads. We are going to find the states where people have volunteered for us. We are going to create an ad that targets each of the other states, and then we are going to create a US map that shows that state highlighted in orange or some other bright color. It would say, for example, "Hey, people of Idaho! We have had volunteers come from twenty-five states, but yours is not one of them. Why don't you come to Lake Charles and help out?" We will also target the church or youth volunteer groups in those states.

We have a good feeling about reaching these goals. For each disaster, we have been able to drive a lot of volunteers to the scene. Here is one thing that we often do, which demonstrates how we use technology to attract volunteers. We watch the reaction to something we have posted on Facebook. If we have sixty-five "likes" in an hour, we think, okay, that is one "like" about every minute.

That's not bad, but if we see that we have 300 Facebook "likes" in a minute, we know that post really connected with people. That is what we want to do most of all—connect with people, touch them, and move them in a way that drives them to help.

It always depends on the purpose of the post. If we are trying to drive volunteers, then we might consider boosting it. However, we would much rather make sure that a post gets seen by a lot of people because it connected with them organically. That is the secret to getting engagement from our followers. If there is something about the way the post is written that people connect with and then respond to, we pay attention to that.

In the four months after Hurricane Laura, we nearly doubled our followers. We figured out this formula for posts that people connect with. They are authentic reactions, and then we can boost the posts. That approach has helped us raise a significant amount of money for helping survivors, and it has driven a good number of volunteers. Technology has enabled us to keep working in Lake Charles and helping more people than we might have without it.

We are primarily a technology movement. We are a platform, and our platform is for people who want to help. It easily enables them to come and be a part of what we do. If we have someone who wants to come and help, and we can give them a place to sleep and can take them where they are needed, that is a big deal. It is all enabled by technology.

Our simple offer of food and a place to stay really helps us get volunteers. Those are expenses that they do not have to take on. If they know that they would have a place to crash, or at least get a meal if they were crashing somewhere else, it makes a huge difference in their willingness and ability to stay for a longer period of time.

We took the time to make sure we could offer that, and it really helped us get and maintain volunteers. If we had to tell people, "Hey, come to Lake Charles, but you have to stay two hours away because there are no hotels or buildings standing," I do not think we would have had the same impact.

We always tell people, "Gas up your car and head out here. We will take care of the rest, or we will figure it out when you get here." That approach has always worked well for us.

Communications and Technology: How We Activate During a Hurricane

The Cajun Navy Ground Force is always looking for innovative ways to connect with citizens to bring disaster relief to those in need. Our Zello channels are one critical way to keep the lines of communication open—not only during and after a specific disaster but also in preparation for the disasters that will inevitably come. The "walkie-talkie" app allows our dispatchers, on-the-ground volunteers, and other good citizens to work quickly and efficiently to share information, plan ahead, and solve problems.

The Zello channels are carefully named to make them easy for anyone to find when searching in the app. Each of the names is approved before being put into use. The app also ties CrowdRelief back to disasters directly. Our channels become the central command for daily operations during and after an event. We also use them to coordinate new volunteers, incoming donations, and supply and rescue requests. Dispatchers use the channels to communicate information about shelters and other resources.

The Cajun Navy Disaster Response Zello channel is our main hub. This is the channel that all future disaster-specific channels are created from. If the engagement falls off on the disaster channels, the main hub is where engagement needs to continue. Our Zello channels have been quite successful. For example, we were excited to find out that we had been the number-one trending channel on Zello for two and a half months following Hurricane Florence.

When a new hurricane or other disaster comes along, the first thing we do is rename the previous disaster's Zello channel based on the new hurricane. We do this because we know that if a storm is coming, that's when the public starts jumping on social media and Zello, searching for that storm name.

As people search, they will usually come across a couple of dozen channels associated with the storm because of the communication that we are putting out. Our goal at that time is to stay in direct contact with the public, educating them about the storm and answering questions that come up. From the Zello channel, we can direct people to register on CrowdRelief to request assistance, to donate supplies or funds, as well as to volunteer.

We have earned a reputation for being reliable. People count on us for information and guidance. Communication with those affected is key. That is how they are able to get the help that they need. When all the other resources are overwhelmed or communication lines are down, we can still use Zello and Facebook to bring relief to the area. We can respond in that way before the big organizations even consider moving in. Without Zello and social media, we would not be able to do what we do so efficiently.

Our lead person on Zello, Shane, does a really good job of getting the word out there. He also posts on Facebook, telling people to come join him on Zello. Just being present makes a big difference. We need somebody on the other end when somebody shows up needing help. When they are reaching out for help and 911 and all emergency services are overwhelmed, they do not know what else to do and they turn to us.

When they get on Zello with hopes of finding somebody on the other end, we will be there for them. With every storm, we go back to the multiple past storm Facebook pages and groups to introduce ourselves again. We start this process as soon as we know the storm is coming. We simply go to the old storm group and pages and let people know that we are activating. We tell them about our new channel and let them know that we are there if they need us.

We do that day after day after day as a storm is approaching. We also use that process after the storm passes. We tell people that we are still here if they need us, that this is our channel, and we just keep spreading the word. Our team wants to reassure them that somebody is still available when others are not yet able to respond, or when the others have packed up and gone home.

This process really does so much good. It allows us to act almost like first responders. The Cajun Navy Ground Force simply would not exist if we did not do these things consistently. Our efficiency can be seen in the numbers. After Hurricane Florence, when we were Zello's number-one trending channel, Zello even interviewed us about how we were using their platform during emergencies. They wanted to know the things we would like to see improved on the app.

These were developers and higher-ups, telling us, "Hey, we know you guys are holding the channel at the top. What are you guys doing? How are you doing it? What's going on? Who are you?" We were able to share who we are, what we do, and how we utilize their platform in disasters. The instant communication that it provides is so powerful. I mean, even the press gets on and monitors what we are saying and doing. That is how the New York Times found us during Hurricane Florence. We were talking on the Zello app, getting the channels set up properly, and then posting on Facebook whenever we were using them. Zello really drives a lot of our activity, and we could not do it without that platform.

Without Zello, there was no instant communication. Obviously, a volunteer who is performing rescues could answer a Facebook request for help with a text message. But it takes time to type out a text message and then get a response. If a volunteer calls that person, it is only a two-way conversation. With Zello being a walkie-talkie app, many on our team can hear and help. Zello shortens the time and the communication in a critical way. I also think that speaking is more efficient at eliminating confusion and also interpreting the situation. When you are having a conversation with somebody, you can really understand what their state of mind is.

Setting up Zello channels and then posting on Facebook has brought us full circle. In 2016, we started off gathering these help requests from Facebook. We moved on to putting the requests (situation, address, and contact number) into a Google spreadsheet that was shared with our dispatchers to send out rescue boaters.

When Hurricane Harvey struck, we were working remotely as well as on-the-ground shifts in a very organized way. We found some uniquely dynamic and driven volunteers who were able to bring the process to a whole new level. We ended up performing more than four thousand rescues, which we documented on our spreadsheets. So that was a real win for what we were trying to accomplish.

It was also during Hurricane Harvey that Laurie Wood from Noggin reached out to us and offered to let us use the Noggin platform. It remains our primary dispatch and data-management platform. We use it for collecting rescue requests and then dispatching individuals to go fulfill those requests. That tool was not really used during Harvey, but we have utilized it extensively for every response since. The Noggin platform really revolutionized how we respond to disasters and made us more effective and efficient.

Combining our dispatch software Noggin with the walkie-talkie app Zello and the GPS app, we basically became citizen first responders with an Emergency Operations Center. We essentially have a 911 system running. We collect rescue requests and then we turn around and dispatch people to go fulfill those requests very efficiently.

We are not trained like normal first responders, and of course, we don't expect to replace them. We supplement them, and we have never intended to be their substitute. The paid first responders make it their career. At the same time, when they are overwhelmed and their systems are not able to respond as effectively or quickly as they need to, we can help fill in the gap for them. And that is what we have done time and time again since 2016. Technology has allowed that to happen.

We might be able to get a few buddies rounded up in boats, but without some data intelligence and communications, we would just spend hours—maybe days—in neighborhoods that have already been evacuated. Without the technology, we would go in blindly. But through technology and social media, we can pretty much pinpoint down to coordinates and an address where somebody can be found or needs assistance.

So technology is the driving force behind what we do. It enables us to respond to incidents with great precision. Without it, the Cajun Navy Ground Force just would not exist. It is important to point that out. As we have always said, our team working remotely is huge and vital. We are a lot more than a bunch of people in boats going around rescuing people.

Chapter 8

Covid-19

When Covid-19 issues emerged in 2020, it became clear that citizens could take specific actions to keep cases down. They included isolating at home, reducing any unnecessary outside activities, and wearing a mask. It's a spreadable virus, despite all of the conspiracy theories. Science has been proven right time and time again throughout this disaster, and the Cajun Navy Ground Force really took a stand.

I spent twenty-six years married to a PhD biochemist, and I interacted with many great scientists over those two and a half decades. So I really respect the science behind Covid.

The CNGF was trying to figure out how to help. We felt that there was an opportunity to really take a role and assist people who were staying home, especially the elderly. Some needed food and prescriptions but were terrified to get out of their houses. These people needed someone to run their errands for them.

We saw an opportunity to use CrowdRelief, our custom disaster platform, to organize such an effort. There were a lot of unknowns at first. It was a novel virus, and new information was coming in moment by moment. We just did not know a lot, except that social distancing would be a good idea. If you could pick things up without getting close to individuals, and then wash your hands, you could transfer those items pretty easily and be okay.

We proposed to a few team leads that this would be a good opportunity to really help our communities in a badly needed way. We thought it could work because we knew we had the tools: the CrowdRelief platform, the ticket system, the dispatch software, the knowledge, and the people. All we needed to do was to move on the idea.

We continued making Facebook posts that encouraged people to mask up. We got a lot of hate on our Facebook page for that. Comments included "Covid is a scam," "it's a plandemic," "it's government control," etc. It was really bad. I would delete a comment and then see that person make another comment, and another. So we would delete all the comments, and then we just blocked the person. That happened time and again. In the end, I just said we will just block you if you make a negative comment at all.

We wound up blocking a huge number of people. We went from about 78,000 to around 70,000 followers on our page, just because of the negative comments. The comments were relentless, because people were so used to the status quo. They did not know how to mentally and emotionally deal with this new virus. It had been decades and decades since the US had to deal with something so difficult. People were not familiar with this, and so they reacted in ways to make themselves feel better.

Covid and its variants have become a very serious issue. So far, there are hundreds of thousands of dead Americans, and the number is growing. This is why the CNGF chose to take a very hard stance.

Unfortunately, before we could get any momentum on setting up a ticket system for Covid assistance, Hurricane Laura struck. But the fact is, the CNGF does hard things. We went out in boats and rescued people, putting ourselves at risk to do it. We certainly did not have all the answers when we hopped in the boats. But we knew that people were in need, and we needed volunteers who understood our vision. We would not ever have all of the answers to achieve our goals, but we would always commit to learning and getting better as we moved forward.

If it had not been for Hurricane Laura, I do believe that our organization would have done some kind of response and relief effort related to the pandemic. But with our volunteer force focused on the storm, all we could do was be vocal on social media. We presented the facts, and even with the blowback, we stood strong. We knew that this information needed to get out, and through social media, we were doing what we thought could save somebody's life.

Only three or four of us were handling social media at that time, and until Laura, we focused on pushing information about the virus. Even today, we are still dealing with it and taking it seriously. We do what we can to prevent the spread of the virus, as we do what we need to do in response to a disaster.

So 2020 was a very interesting year. It was another new learning experience. None of us knew much about Covid in the beginning, and we did not know how bad it was going to be. Then, of course, Louisiana had multiple hurricanes—three back to back to back. It was a very long and draining year, emotionally and physically.

Blocking so many followers from our page was difficult at first. I certainly do not want us to lose followers. But I began to realize that we really did not want those kinds of followers. We did not want or need that drama to interfere with what we are here to do. We do not really want them in our world, whether it is on social media or in the real world. We want people who are aligned with our mission.

This decision actually served us well during Hurricane Laura. Although we had lost 8,000 followers who were vocal naysayers, it became evident that our team had built an amazing platform without all of the negativity. Then when Hurricane Laura came along, our Facebook pages absolutely blew up and we added 60,000 new followers. We learned a really interesting lesson about the importance of finding followers who are aligned with your mission, because it will propel you much farther than the naysayers ever could.

Chapter 9

Hurricane Laura

Laura was a game changer for us for a variety of reasons. It has been referred to as the perfect storm for the Cajun Navy, and it really brought to light what we are capable of. The area that was struck the worst in Southwest Louisiana is my hometown. It is a place that I am familiar with, and as I now live a short distance from Lake Charles, I was able to personally join the boots on the ground responding to this storm. Also, because of Covid, my job had switched to working remotely. Not having to be in the office freed up some time for me.

Laura was more intense than initially recognized, and more importantly, it struck an extremely old, "nothing ever changes" type of community. This relentless hurricane tested the homes in Lake Charles to their limit.

Many of the houses there are between 50 and 100 years old. One major problem is that people do not have mortgages on these older homes, so that often means they do not have insurance on them either. To further complicate the situation, houses in this community have been handed down from family member to family member for generations. People do not leave, so the ownership of the homes can be a convoluted issue. This, in turn, makes dealing with the Federal Emergency Management Agency (FEMA) extremely difficult for the homeowners. You have to show FEMA proof of ownership of the property before they will assist you. It is one of the hurdles you have to clear.

Lake Charles is also isolated in several ways. It is more than an hour from Lafayette by car. This can be a pretty far drive for people who might want to come help after a storm.

There is also a mental divide. The people from Lafayette typically do not go to Lake Charles and vice versa. Lake Charles does not have many relationships with the surrounding cities. The southwest region of Louisiana as a whole is isolated from the rest of the state. Texas, however, is nearby, and having survived Harvey and a near miss with Laura, Texans showered Lake Charles with compassion and aid.

Having helped with Hurricane Harvey so extensively, the Cajun Navy Ground Force is well known and loved in southeast Texas, particularly Houston. The residents have forged this bond with us, and most of our followers come from that area. We were able to target articles and information about Laura there, and that drove a lot of volunteers. It always seems to work when it really matters. The timing was right and people were willing to help.

I had started watching the weather and saw Laura coming. Two days before the storm struck, I went to Beaumont to ride out the storm there and be well positioned to come in and help. On the way, I met a couple of other volunteers who had come down from North Carolina. They, along with two guys from Texas, wanted to join the Cajun Navy and work with us on the ground.

It looked as though the storm was going to hit South Texas, so Beaumont seemed like the best place to be in case we needed to perform rescues. But Laura had a mind of her own and shifted toward Lake Charles. It was August 26, 2020.

A hurricane warning was issued, so we began seeking information about potential problems. If there was flooding, we might not be able to get to Louisiana. I remembered that issue from when we helped during Hurricane Harvey. I decided we should go to Lake Charles the day before the storm was expected to come in.

We could see the clouds gathering as Laura approached. Heading back to Lake Charles, I remembered that I had gotten a call from a guy named Bobby Hunter from the Grand Casino Coushatta in Kinder. He had told me that we could stage in his parking lot, ride out the storm there, and use it in the recovery effort. So I called Bobby and asked if the offer was still available.

"Absolutely!" he responded. So the four volunteers and I all made our way to the Grand Casino Coushatta. When we arrived, Bobby offered me a hotel room to stay in.

Of course, all five of us went to the room. There was no way I was going to stay in a comfortable hotel while they spent the night in the parking lot during a hurricane. This was the night that Laura was going to hit.

Not only did we have the hotel room, but they also gave us the conference room downstairs for our operations. I was really tired and decided I was going to try to get a good night's sleep so I could be prepared for the next day. But I was lying there in bed, watching the hurricane on TV but also the actual storm through the room's large window. The winds were already howling outside. At that time, Laura was striking the Gulf Coast about seventy miles south of us. I decided to get up and go downstairs, and when I made my way down there, everybody else was hanging out there as well.

Under the portico of the hotel, we were just standing around watching the winds bend the trees and the driving rain belt down around us. The local fire department had parked a fire engine in front of the main entrance so the doors would not get blown in. There were probably thirty of us who were waiting and watching the hurricane roll in. Because of the protection of the grand portico, the wind was barely noticeable, and it wasn't raining on us but all around us. It was quite a strange sensation.

Out in the parking lot, we could see the flags on the poles getting tattered by the wind. The palm trees and other tree branches were bent over as if they were blades of grass as Laura approached Kinder from Lake Charles. When it moved into our area, it was still a Category 4, and the winds were incredibly strong. We rode the storm out right there under the portico at the hotel, watching Laura as she battered the parking lot and building.

As the sun finally rose and the winds died down to a mere

breeze, the five of us volunteers jumped into our vehicles and rushed to the gas station to gas up for the journey ahead. We needed full tanks for the trip, but we had not realized it until that moment. With all of the excitement, we had somehow forgotten to do that the night before. Unfortunately, the gas station was closed. We decided to go ahead and load up our gear, and we drove down to Lake Charles.

We started seeing the damage as soon as we pulled out of the hotel. The storm had not been gone for more than an hour, so everything was fresh. Driving down Highway 165 headed to Interstate 10, we encountered multiple trees lying across the road and downed power lines. It caught us off guard for a minute. We had three vehicles—two trucks and a smaller Subaru SUV.

We were able to see pretty far ahead, and at some point we sped up to about fifty-five or sixty miles per hour. Before we knew it, we came upon a damaged power line that we had not been able to see from a distance. It was hanging low, from pole to pole, across the highway. I swerved right to miss it and intuitively slowed down to forty miles per hour. However, the guy behind me did not see the power line in time, and he could not avoid it. He hit it with the grille of his truck.

The impact just ripped the line out of one of the poles, and we all immediately knew that we were lucky it wasn't worse. Because of that accident, we began to see the gravity and danger of the situation, and how careful we needed to be. When we finally made it to I-10, we saw thousands of trees on the side of the road that were standing the night before but now had been snapped in half like twigs. Road signs were mangled and blown everywhere. We had to navigate our way around the destruction on the interstate.

I was really surprised that there was no sign of any authorities anywhere. There were no police officers and no clean-up crew there yet. This was right after the storm, of course, but we really felt completely on our own. With no one else in sight, we kept driving to Lake Charles. I knew precisely where I wanted to go. I had been in contact with other volunteers, and we had planned to meet at the Lake Charles Civic Center. We took the Ryan Street exit in Lake Charles and headed toward our destination.

We could see the downtown area. The buildings were leveled, with debris scattered across the road. We saw the Calcasieu Marine Tower (the Capital One building)—the tall blue glass skyscraper, the only one in Lake Charles. It was later accurately described as looking like Swiss cheese after Laura. More than 40 percent of the windows had been completely blown out and strewn all around and across the road. We had to drive up on the sidewalks and through yards—just whatever we had to do to get where we wanted to go.

At this point, we had no doubt we had to proceed with extreme caution and spread the word to those we came in contact with to stay safe. We took time to stop, take pictures, and share them with our team. This whole time, when we had service, we were in constant contact with our communications team on our Zello disaster response channel. We made sure we kept them abreast of what was going on.

We went around the Calcasieu Marine Tower and pulled into the Civic Center parking lot. We started calling other people to come meet us, and all of these guys began showing up with their boats. This was all very fresh and we had not looked at the city much, but I knew we would not need any boats because of how quickly Hurricane Laura had moved through. It had not dropped a lot of rain over the region, but the winds would have caused the most substantial problems.

I knew immediately that we were going to need chainsaws to tackle the damage. We had brought some but certainly not enough, so I started calling around for more. As we were standing there talking and getting a solid game plan together, I looked out across the lake and noticed black smoke billowing from one of the chemical plants. I drove over to the lakefront and called on our Zello channel to let them know there was a major fire at the plant across the lake on Interstate 10.

Someone listening to our conversation on the channel asked in surprise, "Wait, can you please repeat that?"

I restated that there was a fire at the plant across the lake.

"Thanks for that. Okay," he said. "This is what you are going to do. First, I want you to take a video of it and I want you to send the video to me."

He gave me his email address and told me, "The second thing you're gonna do is you are going to get the fuck out of there! There is probably chlorine gas in the smoke and if you inhale it, it will be instant death."

I looked around at all my volunteers, and they were scrambling to get in their vehicles. It took a minute to rally everybody back together and figure out where to go. We quickly put a game plan together to start helping, and to make sure we did it safely.

I knew where we would go. We would go south—the farthest we could go and still be in southeast Lake Charles. We met up at a gas station on Highway 14, where we immediately began to clear trees and debris. A couple of interesting things happened at that gas station.

While we were regrouping, a lineman in a hardhat wandered up. He introduced himself as Coffee. By this time, we were ready for lunch. I had brought some food and was making sandwiches. I offered one to Coffee, and he stayed there talking and eating with me and my volunteers: D. J. Elan from Beaumont, Texas; Kenny and Jess from North Carolina; and the other Texan. The latter would soon leave with his boat, since water rescues were not needed where we were.

While we were still at the gas station, the second thing that happened was an older gentleman pulled up in his vehicle. He looked as though he had not slept. He got out of his car, walked up, and asked if he could use one of our cellphones. He couldn't charge his in order to make a call.

We charged his phone, and I asked him if he lived in the area.

"Yeah, my house is right around the corner and the roof was ripped off of it," he said.

He had fled his home and ridden out the rest of the storm in his car in this parking lot. I asked him if he would take us to see his house, because maybe we could help him out.

That is what really kicked off our journey. I don't even remember his name, but I did take a picture of him. We went to this gentleman's house and saw that his roof was partially ripped off. We cleaned up all the debris in his driveway to provide some access.

There was not much more we could do for him at that time. We continued down the road that he lived on. A bunch of trees had fallen, blocking a four-way intersection. So we started clearing trees right there on the spot. Coffee, the lineman, was still with us. So now we had six in our group, and we worked together to clear those trees from that intersection and make it passable.

That was our first major accomplishment. There were not any cars driving in the area yet so soon after the storm, but they would come before long. We decided to go find some more trees to clear.

We drove up and down Enterprise Boulevard, the major artery through the heart of Lake Charles. I grew up there. My great-grandmother lived one block from where the six of us were clearing trees. As we surveyed the damage, we saw some National Guardsmen coming in. They offered to let us follow them around and work with them clearing trees.

We accepted and began communicating on our Zello channel with our control, logistics, and communications teams. On that channel, we had the press listening in a lot, and Reuters actually reached out to us. They had heard about the plant fire and wanted a copy of our video. I had shared it on our Facebook page, so I sent them a link to it, and they included the link in an international news story. That drove a lot of awareness of what was happening in Lake Charles.

A BBC reporter called me and wanted her on-the-ground team to ride around with us and interview people. Having worked with the BBC before, we said, "Sure." I brought the BBC team with me on various runs when we were just helping people clear trees.

There were certainly not a lot of cars out the first two days. It was just too dangerous for people to get out, because the roads were still covered with debris and downed power lines. It would remain that way for weeks. The roads were impassable, and there was no electricity or running water. It wasn't possible to pump gas, flush a toilet, take a shower, or buy food. There was no ice, and the weather was scorching hot. You don't typically think about simple amenities such as ice or a shower or even a working bathroom, but if you don't have them, it's a big deal. And none of those things were available. It was like a war zone. There were no resources or services, and that became the norm for about two weeks.

As I was letting the BBC team out of my car in the Prien Lake Mall parking lot, a guy pulled up and asked if I was with the Cajun Navy. I told him I was.

"We heard you guys were in town, and I was wondering if you had a hose replacement for our skid steer," he said.

He asked us because in a situation like this, there is no store open where you can buy supplies. If you need something and did not bring it yourself, there is not much chance you are going to get it. I did not have the part, but I started talking to the guy. He was with a crew of ten guys from Pennsylvania. We decided to team up and work together.

We followed him up to the Walmart on Highway 171, which is in north Lake Charles, and we set up in the parking lot. Once we put the word out that the Cajun Navy was staged there, people started showing up en masse. Multiple chainsaw teams arrived. They also brought food, water, and clothes and just dropped them off for us to distribute in the parking lot. By the end of the first day, we had so much water, food, and supplies that we put the word out to come over if you needed anything at all.

More people showed up. They were the ones who had been affected the most. They were elderly—some who came back from evacuating and others who had stayed nearby and then realized they could not yet get to their homes. These were people now living in their cars, because the only place they had to go was their home. They had lived there their whole lives, and they did not know anybody outside of the city.

They did not have money. There were no open hotels or shelters. So for about the first two weeks, the vast majority of Lake Charles' underserved people were just living in their vehicles. We became their place to go for food and water, to use the bathroom, and to get any kind of assistance that they needed. Lines of cars came through, and we loaded up the trunks with food, water, and supplies. We continued doing that for two long weeks.

During that time, we also ran crews very efficiently, clearing roads. We broke transport down into grids, and we organized the teams to work a grid. We had one guy going among the teams, keeping everybody moving, so that they could work as efficiently and as long as possible. These guys got going at eight or nine in the morning and worked until five or six. We would run lunch and supplies to them as needed.

One of the most interesting stories I remember hearing about from my girlfriend, Camille, provides an example of what people were dealing with. A woman drove up with a tree hanging out of her back windshield, dragging on the ground.

"Ma'am, we can take that tree out for you. Did you know this is free?" Camille asked her.

The woman told her not to touch it. She was worried that her insurance company would not believe her and help her unless they saw the tree for themselves. Our group loaded up the backseat with water, food, and supplies. And that tree was still sticking out the back of her car as she drove off.

When the crews would come back from clearing trees out in the community, they would bring all types of pets that people had left behind. We had bunnies, turtles, plenty of dogs and cats—just about every kind of living thing you could imagine. The crews would not even think of abandoning these pets. With all these animals coming, we put out a call for cages, and people would show up with some.

Remember, I had gone to Beaumont by myself two days before the storm. The day before Laura, I arrived at the hotel in Kinder with four volunteers. Then the next day, we had dozens and dozens more, because we shared on Facebook what we were doing and what our needs were. By the time two weeks passed, we had probably over three hundred volunteers working with us out of that parking lot, feeding people. More than 120 guys with chainsaws worked in the Goosport area of Lake Charles, and they cleared every single road.

We had an abundance of supplies dropped off at the Walmart by concerned citizens driving in to help. At some point, somebody brought a gooseneck trailer to keep the supplies out of the weather. We don't even know where it came from. We loaded the entire trailer with water. An eighteen-wheeler also showed up, full of water. We had to turn it away because there was no way we could handle it.

Exxon donated two generators to us that we still have today. That was all during the first two weeks. From there, we set up in downtown Lake Charles outside a restaurant where we served people. They were coming and going, trying to repair their homes and work on their streets. We did that for eighteen days.

I had taken personal time to work in Lake Charles, and then my employer gave me two more weeks off to continue. They knew what I did. I told them what was happening, and I explained that the help was badly needed. The residents of Lake Charles needed people who had experience organizing and executing a disaster response. The problem is those people are employed because they are capable. The employers have to recognize that their skilled people can contribute at a time like this. My employer recognized that and gave me the additional time. As my leave was ending, I put some other volunteers in charge, and they really stepped up.

During our time at the restaurant, we served 55,000 meals. We started off just serving walkups. But soon drivers were stopping on the road and asking if they could take some food with them. So we would pass it to them through their car window. It occurred to me that with all these cars coming, we could ramp up our operation and really blow this thing up. We turned our tables to face the road and set up tents.

We established two stations where we would stack up the meals, and we had a volunteer-led production line going in the back. As a car would pull up, someone would hand the food through the window and then keep that vehicle moving. The traffic would get backed up quite a bit, since this was on Ryan Street, a main thoroughfare. Ryan Street, by the way, is named for my great-great-great-great-great-grandfather, John Jacob Ryan. He was the "Father of Lake Charles." And the Calcasieu Marine Tower, the blue building that had the glass blown out of it? The construction company on my mom's side of the family built it.

These ties definitely give me a reason to stay and help. I feel a real sense of family there. I grew up there, and my mom died in Lake Charles when I was thirteen. She took her own life. I lived with her there in Lake Charles at the time. These are the reasons why I call Laura the perfect storm. This place held a special meaning for me.

An enormous generator, large enough to power several buildings, was donated to us to run the whole restaurant. The restaurant was set up for us completely free because of what we were doing to serve the community. We had a number of volunteers helping us, and at times, we were serving more than five thousand people a day.

That is not an easy thing to do. We had to be prepared. So at night, when we were done serving everyone, we would plan what to serve the next day. We had to start that process early enough to be able to either purchase the food we would need or have it donated.

One time, somebody brought us 36,000 bags of potato chips. I think it was 600 cases. It was so much that we were giving away potato chips for the next four months.

We did not have anywhere to store all the food donations at the time, so a lot of the cardboard boxes got stacked outside the restaurant. Then we realized we had to keep them covered so they did not get rained on. I was also kind of worried that we might lose our generator, so I leased a refrigerated eighteen-wheeler truck and parked it around the back for ten days just in case. So much planning and coordination was required to keep everything running smoothly.

Of course, we had to clean up the restaurant before we used it. It was an okay building but not clean by any means. It was not damaged by the storm, but the walk-in refrigerator had not been cleaned out ahead of time, and they had not had power for almost fourteen days. The refrigerator was a smelly gooey mess, but our team of volunteers cleaned it out so that we could use it. That refrigerator was probably the most important and useful thing that we possessed at that moment.

We had to assess what we had available. We had the refrigerator, we had the ability to wash dishes, and we had the generator. Those things were critical. We also had air conditioning, which was important because this was in August and early September. It was still 90 to 100 degrees outside and extremely humid. The air conditioning gave the volunteers a chance to get out of the heat, so that worked out well.

During this time, we were still clearing roads and helping people clear trees from homes. We also purchased a big tent and set it up in a parking lot to receive and distribute donated supplies. Just like in the Walmart parking lot, people would drive up, we would load up their cars with supplies, and they would be on their way.

Between August 27 and September 26, we were sending out crews of guys every day with chainsaws to clear trees from roads and people's homes, running the supply drive, and keeping the restaurant rolling—and we did it 100 percent with volunteers.

At that point, we made the decision to let the restaurant go. We felt that we had accomplished all we could there. For the next phase of our operation, we leased a building across from the restaurant to serve as a volunteer headquarters and supply center.

This whole time, Lake Charles still did not have electricity. It took six weeks—early October—for power to be restored. The whole city was under a curfew during that time. Residents and volunteers had to be out of Lake Charles by 8:00 P.M. each day. So we had to get all our work done and then head back to the Grand Casino Coushatta.

Volunteers would come and go at any given time. On a typical day, we fed and housed between fifteen and forty volunteers at that hotel. We had the conference room and one guestroom with two queen-size beds. We let the girls stay in the guestroom, and the guys slept on the floor in the conference room.

This whole time, yes—Coffee was still with us. Coffee the lineman would come and hang out with us when he got off work. He is also a musician, and I learned that he had actually opened for Chris Stapleton. So I bought him a guitar, and he played for us one night down in the conference room.

I managed to get an infection in both eyes from sleeping on the floor. It got so bad that my girlfriend drove me at 2:00 A.M. to the emergency center in Oakdale, a very small town north of Kinder. The interstate and backroads still had no lights, so we had to navigate our way in complete darkness.

I will never forget the number of our guestroom at the Grand Casino Coushatta. I do not know if it was fortuitous or on purpose, but we ended up in Room 316—as in John 3:16. So we always had that Bible verse in the back of our minds. John 3:16 says, "For God so loved the world that he gave his one and only Son, that whoever believes in him shall not perish but have eternal life."

We were in this hotel for about five weeks, and we had over 250 volunteers come and go there. Everyone used the shower in that guestroom, and many people brought their own brand of shampoo, conditioner, and soap. I always laughed because there were probably thirty bottles in that shower! It was definitely an interesting time.

Eventually, the hotel management said, "Look, you guys are going to have to go."

We know that we had overstayed our welcome a little bit, but we ended on a good note. They were very appreciative of what we were doing, but I could not blame them for wanting their guestroom and conference room back. So I decided we could just live at our new headquarters, at 710 Ryan Street. That became our command center for the next six months.

We just continued our operations, clearing trees, serving food, and giving away donations. People kept dropping off food, water, and clothes at our headquarters. We had a sign made and put it at the top of the building so everybody would know where the Cajun Navy Ground Force was located.

I do not know how many tons of food, clothes, baby formula, diapers, notebooks, shoes, blankets, and countless other items we gave away. But I do know that none of it ever went to waste. Thousands and thousands of items were dropped off, things that we would just turn around and give away.

We decided to do something innovative. We partnered with a Lake Charles company called Gophr. You can download the app and then shop from various stores in Lake Charles. A driver will pick those items up from multiple stores and bring them to you.

We worked with Gophr to create our own "store" on the app, except everything was free. You could select anything you needed, within a certain limit. Then a Gophr driver would pick it up at our headquarters and deliver it to you. We thought it was a good way to keep crowds from coming into the headquarters during the Covid pandemic.

We had many volunteers sleeping inside the building. Some would wake up and go into the community to clear trees from homes and repair them. Others would stay and work inside our supply center, making sure people got the things they needed. They filled the Gophr orders and got the boxes ready for the drivers. I knew that we would be able to stay busy helping people in small ways.

People do not realize that disasters leave entire communities in crisis. They may say, for example, that ten people were killed but everybody else lived, so everything is okay. But it is not! Those tens of thousands of people who survived are still left in a major crisis, and they need help.

I don't really refer to an event like this as just a disaster anymore. It is much more than that. When you hear the word "disaster," you think of a short event. But a disaster leads to a crisis for many people, and we need to talk about it long term.

We have many organizations designed to help in a natural disaster, but they respond during the disaster and then maybe a week or so after it. I liken the situation to going to the emergency room. Doctors will see you briefly and provide the immediate treatment, but they have to go quickly from patient to patient. Nurses, however, are hands on. They are the ones who really make sure you are comfortable and take care of you.

We do not typically have "nurses" in the disaster industry. We have a lot of "doctors." The Cajun Navy Ground Force has filled the role of nurses. We stay behind and check on the "patients" every day, making sure they are doing okay. That piece has been missing from the disaster world. It needs the kind of assistance that we are able to bring.

We are not really specialists, but you do not need a specialist to put a case of water in somebody's trunk or deliver it to them. You do not need an expert to hand out boxes of diapers. There is no special training required. Being hands on is the unique value that we bring to this disaster ecosystem, and we are able to do it in big ways, just as we did in Lake Charles.

We completely funded ourselves by telling stories on Facebook and asking people to donate. During all of this, if I spotted something that inspired me, I would get on Facebook and write a story right then. Then I would add a link for people to help by volunteering or donating. It worked, and people responded in a big way.

Our group has a knack for spotting stories that are worth telling. I wrote one called "The City with No Lights." An elderly woman had come up to our supply depot in the parking lot behind our headquarters. She was very disabled, and she had a real deer-in-the-headlights look on her face. All she wanted was a flashlight. So I asked her why.

"Because at night when our generators run out of gas, it's completely dark in my home," she told me, "and there are no streetlights, there's no electricity, and I just don't want to be in the dark if I need to go to the bathroom or need to get around in my home. Not only me, but all of my neighbors are having the same problem."

So I gave her a whole bunch of flashlights, then looked out over the city and thought about it. I now saw the situation in a whole new way, from the perspective of people like her just living day to day. Lake Charles was the city with no lights.

That one article had over 2.5 million views, and it was shared 2,000 times in one day. It raised $80,000 for our efforts. I could not believe people responded in that way. Telling stories is what is important, and it is how we get funded to help people.

Our group was able to purchase a badly damaged house so that we could rehab it for our volunteers to have a place to live. For eight or nine months, our volunteers had been using one shower and had no beds or sheets. They were still sleeping on air mattresses. In order to keep volunteers around, you have to provide some comforts. They need a sense of normality at some point, and that house really let us give them that.

This crisis is worse than Hurricane Harvey, which flooded 154,000 homes. With Hurricane Laura, 500,000 properties were damaged, but it was a wind disaster. Roofs were ripped off, walls were caved in, and homes were completely destroyed. They just do not exist anymore. Other houses and apartment complexes were left uninhabitable.

So both hurricanes damaged tens of thousands of homes, but wind devastation can be much worse than flooding, because it requires more than replacing sheetrock. You have to repair your roof, and because of the age of these homes, many people did not have mortgages. They did not have insurance, and so months and years later, countless homes in Lake Charles still had blue tarps on them.

When it rains, it rains in their homes. I know that is a fact, because people are still messaging me for help. And during the summer, temperatures over ninety degrees result in mold from all that moisture. It is black mold, which can scar your lungs if you are exposed to it for very long. Basically, all these homes that have not been repaired are uninhabitable.

Throughout all of this, the Cajun Navy Ground Force's motto became "Under Promise and Over Deliver." I took the time to walk up to every volunteer, introduce myself, and have a conversation. I created an instant rapport with every person coming in. I would say that, yes, things will get hard and even overwhelming. When they do, stay positive and let it go.

I do that because disasters are negative by nature. People are in a major crisis, and the only way to combat that is with positivity. Even the smallest positive thing you do leads to something else positive, and that leads to a bigger positive. So no matter what, stay 100 percent positive through every single thing you encounter. Positive energy is the only way to fight the negative energy created by these natural disasters.

After years of helping disaster survivors, we have gathered more stories than we can count. They are stories of hopelessness but also strength, resilience, and community. I would like to share some of those stories with you. These are just a few examples of the work we do with the community, and the people who keep us going—no matter what.

Chapter 10

Survivor Stories

Mrs. Strickland's Story

When people and organizations work together, the possibilities are endless. Following Hurricane Florence in September 2018, Cajun Navy Ground Force (CNGF) and the North Carolina Baptists on Mission were able to team up to help a victim in need.

CNGF had received a message from a worried mom. Mrs. Strickland's pregnant daughter's home was full of toxic mold, and she wasn't expecting help from her landlord. She was living in the home with her four-year-old son and feared that they might be evicted if she pushed the issue.

A CNGF volunteer referred the woman to the CrowdRelief website to submit a ticket to connect the family with the resources they needed. Someone connected the young woman with Baptists on Mission. By that night, she and her child were relocated; and by the next morning, Baptists on Mission were on their way to her home to help.

Mrs. Strickland said that she was overwhelmed by the love and kindness they had shown to her family. She sent a thank-you message to the volunteer who helped her.

She wrote, "There were so many people all around me who were desperate and needed help. The people of Wilmington and people from all over the country have stepped up and embraced their neighbors, even while they struggled with their own loss and destruction. In the midst of all this heartbreak, there is still joy."

A New Heartbreak

This story is by Robin Hall, one of our Cajun Navy Ground Force members. She drove to Louisiana from Maine after Hurricane Laura because she could see the needs and how few people were serving in this overwhelming crisis. . . .

Every day here I hear a new story, learn a new heartbreak, see a new plea for hope. But today . . . today I was hit harder than normal.

A seventy-two-year-old man . . . Living in his garage. Sleeping on a line of "five-inch-thick couch cushions.

His home destroyed, he has battled two hurricanes, a winter storm, an insurance company, and lost his job. At an age when he should be living life kicking back on a beach, this man is sleeping on cushions in a garage in temperatures that headed over a hundred, with no air conditioning.

All I could offer him today was an ear to listen, a hand to hold, a little help installing a small AC unit, an air mattress, sheets, new pillows, and a case of water. In return, he offered me a smile, a thank-you, and a genuine kind spirit that will stick with me for a long time.

Where is our humanity when we, as a "civilized society," continue to turn a blind eye? To allow our elderly, our veterans, our disabled, to find themselves in these conditions? I spent fifteen minutes in that garage and walked out soaked in sweat. I mean soaked. I actually wrung the sweat out of my shirt and hair. This man has been living like that. It makes me mad, sad, and just numb all at the same time.

Tonight I will obsess about this and try to think of ways to help him. Tomorrow, I will go visit and hope he found some relief from the heat and was able to finally have a good night's sleep. And going forward I will continue to ask, "How in the hell do we allow this to happen?"

Mrs. Michael's Story

This is a message posted by Mrs. Michael, one of the survivors we assisted early on when services in Lake Charles were completely shut down. . . .

I wanted to share a different kind of Cajun Navy story with you. Please share to all of the other volunteers and anyone else who you think should hear it.

Last fall when you guys first showed up—man, were we happy to see you! Y'all were such a blessing to Samiyah, Wyatt, me, and our yellow Lab baby, Lamar. Between Laura and Delta, I went to New Orleans to pick up Samiyah and Wyatt's almost five-month-old baby sister, who had been in the NICU there since her birth last May. She came home on a very specialized, expensive, and nearly impossible-to-find formula, with tons of tummy and health issues. At almost five months she weighed less than eight pounds and had just gotten big enough to wear preemie clothes and preemie extra-small diapers.

The Cajun Navy stepped in to help and got us not just the help we needed but items we needed too: baby formula that cost sixty-five dollars a can, and she took two a week!

Fast forward to now. Emily turned one on May 29. And she went for her twelve-month checkup yesterday. She now weighs seventeen pounds, wears a size one diaper and is heading towards a size two. She wears size three- to six-month clothes. She still can't wear shoes because they don't make them small enough, but she is working on it. She can sit and stand on her own and can walk short distances by herself. She says and waves "hey" and "bye-bye,"; she says, "Mama"; loves to dance. She is learning to say and sign "please," "thank you," "milk," "juice," and "eat."

She has the growth pattern of a normal one-year-old. She has a few teeth and is cutting more. She is eating solid foods, and they said after this last container of formula, she can switch to regular whole milk and PediaSure for the extra calories. She got a great bill of health, especially considering all that she has been through.

None of this—*none* of it—would have been possible without the love and generosity of the Cajun Navy and all of the wonderful donors and volunteers. Wyatt rarely has seizures anymore and is now verbal. He knows letters, colors, shapes, and numbers and can count, add, subtract, and spell simple words and his name.

Samiyah received so many awards I am going to have to get three totes to put them all in. She was able to go back to school in person and start her school year on grade level (she had been three grade levels behind), made honor roll for the first time in her life, and did it twice. She received "outstanding behavior" every single day (we had been getting bad reports every single day before). She got perfect attendance. She gets to start sixth grade taking high-school courses. She took ballet and tap this year, went from a beginner to level 3 with other girls her age within months, and received a prima ballerina award.

Lamar (the dog) has gained back all of the weight he lost due to anxiety through the storms.

In all, I want you to know that we could not have done it, none of it, if it weren't for all that the Cajun Navy is. It's been a rough year for sure, but as bad as it has been—and it has been bad—we still have so much to be thankful for.

And . . . it gets better! The kids have all been with me through the foster-care system. Samiyah and Wyatt have been cleared and I have been certified to adopt them. Emily should be cleared as well in October. Big adoption party when we get it!

So, I won't bother you as I know that you are busy slaying dragons and rescuing damsels in distress and such. I just wanted to say thank you from all of us, and for all that you do for us, and for all of our neighbors near and far. May God bless you and keep you, each and every one. Big Cajun Navy hugs from my little family to you and all the others. Thank you.

Better Together

Working together truly is better. We got a call from a mother in need, and a couple of the team headed her way while the others went to tarp a roof. When the team came down from the roof, the lady they were serving came out and said, "Wait, I have things for that family you did a video about!"

These people were served and now they were serving. They loaded us up with an air conditioner and appliances for us to deliver to two households in need. We already had a plan to deliver food for the Vessel Project, so we got some hot meals and continued rolling.

We got a call from a local church that a ninety-year-old woman was in need of a washer and dryer. Now was our chance to reach out to a community member who had offered those appliances. We picked them up and delivered them with some hot food to her and her family.

From there, we went to Mill Street Church of Christ to help unload a semi full of pews that came in from Austin, Texas, after Mill Street's were ruined by the floods. Leaving the church, we received a text that someone had a refrigerator in Sulphur for the man in our live video that morning. We were already heading that way to deliver the air conditioner unit we received in the morning to a man who had been sleeping outside with a fan, because the heat in his camper was so unbearable. We picked up that refrigerator and came back to Lake Charles, delivering more to those in need.

So much happened that day, and it all started with a call for help. We posted the story and our community answered. We are so proud to be on the ground serving our community alongside everyday people and organizations. It takes a village.

Mrs. Christine's Story

The story of Mrs. Christine is another example of how the system has failed fragile people in our community. In February 2021, the Cajun Navy found Mrs. Christine, a ninety-two-year-old woman, living in her car for two months after losing her home to Hurricane Laura.

After seeing Mrs. Christine's story, our amazing volunteer Robin drove all the way from Maine to Louisiana to help out. Together with volunteers from Houston and New Orleans, Robin and team leader Becky Johnson started cleaning out Mrs. Christine's house in March. It was the first step to getting this lovely lady back in her own home! In the meantime, Becky opened up her home to Mrs. Christine, so she would have a safe place to live while the team worked on her house.

Mrs. Christine got to visit her badly damaged home regularly—the home in which she had lived for half a century. Her house was uninsured, and she was worried about not being able to live there anymore.

In mid-April, a local business stepped up to the challenge and surprised Mrs. Christine by starting repairs on her roof! We all knew that Mrs. Christine was coming by for her regular visit, but we wanted to surprise her and didn't let her know what we were doing. She didn't expect to see the badly needed repairs on her damaged roof happening in real time right before her eyes when she turned the corner! Overwhelmed, she broke down in tears when she saw the activity on her roof. It's understandable that after so many months of extreme stress, she could not stop the flood of emotions.

Four months after rescuing Mrs. Christine from living in her car, we started the repair work on her home. Our team encountered several problems, including a huge beehive in the walls, but we made great strides. As the repairs continued, Mrs. Christine still lived with Becky, and she and her daughter Myra felt incredibly grateful for everyone who was helping.

Mrs. Christine's newfound hope is what keeps us going!

Mrs. Seaberry's Story

We received a lovely message from Mrs. Seaberry after our team helped her son clean up his property. It is another example of how community support can bring strangers together! . . .

This has been an amazing week. My son Jerome Seaberry, Jr., was denied by his insurance company for the hurricane damages, so his yard has been in disarray since Hurricane Laura hit. A few months ago I called the Cajun Navy and spoke to Marissa. She guaranteed that she would find Jerome some help. Well, two months later, she kept her word. This group of wonderful people drove down from Illinois to help families here with hurricane recovery and they were assigned to my son.

When they saw the devastation of his property, they didn't hesitate to clean it up. When Jerome called me to tell me of his blessing, immediately in my spirit I decided to cook for them. I cooked red beans, sausage, rice, smothered chicken, and cornbread. They were so grateful and hungry! While visiting with them it dropped in my spirit again to make them a gumbo. So tonight I brought it to them.

The evening was beautiful. God showed up.

I sat in a house full of volunteers who love the Lord, sharing food for the physical body and food for the spirit. We had a jam session while the pastor played his guitar and we all sang along. It's amazing how no matter where you live or what state you are from, the spirit of God knows all and makes strangers become friends instantly. We all sat there laughing and singing and enjoying the Word of God!

Thank you, everyone!

Miss Etta's Story

One of the stories that will always stay with me is the story of Miss Etta. While she didn't get to enjoy her cleaned and repaired home for long, we are honored that we were able to help her feel at home and safe again during the last days of her life. Miss Etta will always have a special place in our hearts.

In her younger years, Miss Etta was the life of the party. She was strong, proud, and quick-witted. Since her passing, others have told me stories that would make you raise a glass to a woman well loved and a life well lived. For that reason, it was difficult for me to comprehend the conditions she was living in, almost a year after the 2016 Great Louisiana Flood, and no one was helping her.

Eight months after the flood, we heard of sixty-seven-year-old Miss Etta's situation and went to her house. Until recently, I just couldn't bring myself to publicly show what the inside of her home looked like, which, after sitting like that for so long, was in a really bad state and extremely unhealthy. Frankly, she was embarrassed about it—and who wouldn't be? After all, a woman's home is her castle, and it was no different for Miss Etta. She just had nowhere to turn for help.

When I met her, this physically frail but mentally strong woman kept telling me she had it under control and really didn't need much help. Of course, I knew differently and started the wheels turning to rebuild her home.

We gathered a team of twenty-five volunteers from twelve different nonprofits and spent a full day cleaning up and repairing the damage left by three feet of water. Miss Etta didn't want to throw anything away. Probably like for most of you, her possessions and keepsakes connected her to her past. Anyone who has faced flood damage knows how absolutely heart-wrenching the cleaning process is. You are left to pick and choose what water-damaged memories to save or throw away.

To help her through the process of cleaning out her home, we sat her in a chair outside and patiently walked each possession past her so she could decide what to keep and what to let go. If she decided to keep something, we placed it in her garage. If she said to throw it away, we went straight to the dumpster sitting out front.

At one point somebody uncovered a princess crown. When they walked up to her with it . . . she immediately grabbed it and put it on her head. The crown stayed there for the duration of the day, right where it belonged, no doubt evoking memories of past loves. Not long after she placed the crown on her head, Miss Etta beckoned me over. When I asked her what she wanted, she pointed at her possessions, and fighting back tears, she made the difficult call of saying to just throw it all away.

We spent the day cleaning out the home, repairing the outside, and installing sheetrock and new cabinets. At lunchtime, one of our volunteers arranged for Baton Rouge blues singer Kenny Neal to come and play guitar for Miss Etta and all the volunteers.

The day finished with the volunteers saying their goodbyes and leaving Miss Etta with a clean, healthy house. There was still work to be done, but we coordinated various contractors to finish over the next couple of weeks.

Three days later, we returned to bring some things that were donated for her, such as a couch and television. One of our volunteers noticed her dog running around in the front yard. When the volunteer went into the freshly completed home, she found Miss Etta passed away inside. The volunteers who had shown so much compassion and had just left were heartbroken, as were her family and everyone who knew her.

Talking to her family afterward, we learned that Miss Etta had told them that the day the community showed up to help her rebuild her home was the biggest day of her life. For me it was a moment of pride knowing that any citizen, regardless of occupation, can reach out and touch someone.

If you look at where this organization is now, you might feel like an outsider, like we're a large, professionally organized group. The truth is, when we got started, we did not have any idea what we were doing. We did not have special access or information or even any resources beyond what was in our own bank accounts.

But it did not matter. We got started anyway and figured it out as we went. And there is always room for you.

Most of us go through our lives routinely, going to work, enjoying the weekend, spending time with family. We saw the Great Louisiana Flood as a unique opportunity to serve our fellow man. Opportunities such as this present themselves very rarely, and for every person we touched, we were changed as well.

There is no reason you cannot do the same. That is the spirit of the Cajun Navy Ground Force; we are all just citizens stepping up to help. The same Cajun Navy that dispatched boaters to rescue tens of thousands showed up to help Miss Etta rebuild her home. And by doing so, the Cajun Navy ensured that Etta Sharolyn Daughdrill lived her final days as a princess, who was once again in her castle.

Thank you, Miss Etta, for teaching us to never quit!

Mr. Joe's Story

In May 2021 we heard about Joe, a homeless veteran who had walked from Jennings to Lake Charles in the hope of finding help. As soon as we found out, our team member Becky went out and drove around town, looking for him. She had already been out all day, nonstop, helping to clean out homes, deliver supplies, and more. Yet she managed to find him!

We were able to contact his family in Atlanta and started moving to help him get there.

Joe told us that before he left Louisiana, he only wanted two things: some gumbo and to hear the song "Cajun Blood." Gumbo was not a problem—we got the roux burning and smelling up the house in no time! As far as the song goes, we had a *huge* surprise for Joe at Rikenjaks Brewing Company in Lake Charles. Jo-EL Sonnier II himself met with Joe and played for him, as a thank-you for his service.

The day after that, Joe flew off to spend time with his family in Atlanta. He thanked us for the help and the kind words and said he would do it all over again just to meet us! While we are all happy and thankful for Joe, his story is just one of countless others that show the system is broken and leaves our most vulnerable to fend for themselves.

These are just some of the stories that we encounter every day. And these people are the lucky ones—we found them and helped them rebuild their lives. It breaks my heart to think about the countless people out there, including the elderly and veterans who have risked their lives for this country, who have fallen through the cracks.

I like to say that the Cajun Navy Ground Force is the safety net for people who have fallen through the safety net. We try to find and help these people as much as we can, but we can't do it without you. We need volunteers. We need funding. Without it, the Cajun Navy Ground Force cannot exist, and these people will have no one to fall back on.

Hurricanes will continue to batter Louisiana and other parts of the country. People will lose their homes and their livelihoods. But this is our home, our community, and it always will be. With your help, we will be here for every single storm, ready to offer assistance whenever and wherever it is needed. As long as there are people who need us, people such as Miss Etta, Mr. Joe, and Mrs. Christine, we won't quit.

Appendix A

Cajun Navy Standard Operating Procedures and Processes for Volunteers

The Cajun Navy Ground Force is always working to streamline the processes we use in all aspects of our organization. We believe that by setting firm guidelines that can be used to train volunteers and to establish routines, we can save time and operate more effectively overall. The following processes are a work in progress and will be updated as we learn and grow.

Background

Cajun Navy Ground Force founder Rob Gaudet worked as a systems engineer for twenty-five years, building business systems and making them more efficient. He applied his knowledge and experience to disaster relief in 2016 when he founded the organization as a means of citizen-led disaster relief driven by volunteers utilizing technology. During a crisis, members of CNGF collaborate to create innovative ways for citizens to meet specific needs of disaster survivors quickly and efficiently. The Cajun Navy team is made up of professionals with years of experience delivering technology, business software, social media, logistics, and marketing solutions. Safety protocol is essential in all operations and is ensured by implementing Standard Operating Procedures, by working alongside local authorities, and by putting our rigorous vetting process into practice.

The Cajun Navy management team has a proven record of leadership through the execution of plans that have achieved desired outcomes. Most recently, we have had between eight and twelve teams dispatched to Lake Charles, Louisiana, leading recovery efforts and feeding thousands of Hurricane Laura survivors each day. We then transitioned to securing tarps on roofs and cutting trees off of homes to enable hurricane victims to safely return to their homes.

Cajun Navy Ground Force has continued to build relationships with other organizations and individuals that share our' vision for citizen-led disaster relief. With the right partners, we believe the sky's the limit for future citizen-led efforts. We envision a model where disaster funds will be raised not only for the immediate needs following a disaster but also for the difficult work of long-term recovery.

Overview of Cajun Navy's Standard Operating Procedures for Disaster Relief

Purpose: Cajun Navy Ground Force has established a disaster SOP to document the policies, procedures, and information related to operations during a disaster. The SOP is a vital planning tool to ensure that formal agreements and partnerships with state emergency management, volunteers, and other associates are executed effectively. The SOP is reviewed annually and updated with any changes to agreements, roles, responsibilities, and capabilities.

Concept of Operations: Cajun Navy Ground Force is an action-oriented think tank consisting of a diverse group of technology, social media, disaster relief, and rescue professionals. As a 501(c)(3) charity, our objective is to empower communities across the country with the knowledge of how to use technology, social media, and mobile apps to take action in their own communities in the midst and aftermath of a disaster. We are working together to understand how to fill the gaps during the chaos of disaster and respond more quickly than authorities are typically able to. In the aftermath, our greatest opportunities lie in rebuild and recovery efforts.

As we continue to learn from experience and adapt to the ever-changing nature of technology, we recognize that our volunteers are our greatest assets. With extensive and diverse backgrounds, strengths, and abilities, we strive to maximize our collective impact by engaging volunteers where they are most needed. In our organization, people bring their talents to the table and use them in ways that complement one another.

Preparedness and Training: Cajun Navy volunteers come from diverse backgrounds and areas of expertise. Each person is matched with a team determined by their knowledge, skills, and preferences. Experienced team leaders take on the responsibility of training volunteers for specific roles and for cross training them in other areas. During the off-season, volunteers may participate in educational experiences by using hypothetical scenarios, by viewing training videos created by team leaders, and through one-on-one sessions with seasoned volunteers.

Notifications and Triggers for Activation: Core Team members follow the weather and make appropriate assessments of a situation to determine whether or not to activate a plan. Teams are created, reorganized, and maintained in preparation for an imminent event. The Core Team, consisting of members of all teams, determines when to activate Cajun Navy relief efforts. The need for evacuation, overwhelmed 911 operations, and contact from citizens requesting assistance are often the first events that trigger activation.

Emergency Functions: We have divided disaster recovery into seven phases. During each phase, the roles of each team may change but are essential. Timing is important in meeting the needs of survivors of disasters. The phases are:

Prepare: Preparedness focuses on understanding how a disaster might impact the community and how education, outreach, and training can build capacity to respond to and recover from a disaster. During the preparation phase, the Social Media Team is busy monitoring Facebook posts, verifying and sharing pertinent resources and information, and watching for incoming messages. The Dispatch Team works on getting volunteer dispatchers on board and starts a list of local contacts and resources. The Core Team works with local authorities to offer assistance and coordinate rescue plans, so that dispatching can begin immediately.

Evacuate and Shelter: During these phases, the Cajun Navy encourages those being asked to evacuate to leave. For those who choose not to leave, we ask them to download the CNGF app and let us know they are staying behind. We can see where they are, and the app will send them dire warnings that their life is in danger. There is also a countdown to when they will not be able to leave.

The Social Media Team disseminates information about steps to take before evacuating, shelters that accept pets, and other essential resources. They answer questions and direct people to resources. The team leader for ground support establishes contact with the team they are working with as well as with someone local to enable rapid egress from the area. The Animal Rescue Team connects people with temporary shelters for pets, and the Mapping Team adds resources on Google as they are established. The Zello Team provides information to listeners and answers questions. The Vetting Team vets incoming volunteers. The Core Team continues to monitor the situation and establish imminent needs.

Rescue: As soon as it is safe, any needed rescues would begin. Volunteers pull tickets that come in and work with communication teams to make sure Facebook, Messenger, and Zello requests get entered as tickets. Tickets then get called to verify and gather more information, updated in Noggin, and moved from "Open" to "Verified" status.

Teams are dispatched based on locations. Volunteers on the ground are required to follow all established safety measures, and they must remain in communication with dispatch. Separate channels are used between ground and dispatch for security purposes, and GPS helps monitor those on the ground. All identifying survivor information is kept confidential.

Transition: After the disaster, volunteers register through CrowdRelief, an online platform to connect volunteers, survivors, and resources. As the Social Media Team communicates with other teams to determine what is needed, they put out Facebook posts to ask for volunteers, donations, and supplies.

Replenish and Rebuild: Immediately following a disaster, we establish staging areas to dispense food, water, and supplies and to provide hot meals for disaster survivors. We muck out and clean up homes, tarp roofs, and cut trees off of houses to enable families to return to their homes. We believe that with the right partners, the possibilities are endless for future rebuild efforts. We anticipate the day when disaster funds will be raised not only for essential needs of survivors following a disaster but also for the arduous work of long-term recovery.

Coordination and Organization: Cajun Navy Ground Force teams serve distinct purposes within the organization. The teams are organized as follows.

Core Operations: The Core Team consists of team leaders. The team collaborates to establish procedures, discuss issues that arise, and solve problems. Team leaders communicate information from the Core Team to their individual team members.

Social Media: Social media is often our first interaction with the public. People come to us online for answers or to offer help. Team members answer everyday questions and direct people about where to donate or take supplies. They verify any rescue requests posted on pages or groups.

The Social Media Team shares helpful information on Facebook pages and in groups. Volunteers direct people to CrowdRelief and Zello, as well.

Dispatch Operations: Dispatch volunteers enter tickets in Noggin for supply or rescue requests. They work with boots on the ground (BOGs) to get them to where a rescue or supply request needs to be filled, and they follow a ticket through to close it. Dispatch volunteers listen on Zello for people with needs and assist them. For example, if someone is on Zello and is distraught during a storm, a dispatcher will calm them and get the info needed to submit a ticket for them.

Emergency Management: Before deployment, this team makes contact with the local government to see what help is needed that we can provide through the resources that we have.

Animal Rescue: The Animal Rescue Team posts animal rescue needs on social media. Team members network with other groups to communicate information about rescues taking place and other animal needs.

Mapping: The Mapping Team adds resource info to a Google map that can be accessed on different levels. BOGs have their own map for resources available to them while in the field, such as hot food, lodging, and other locations they can use for staging. The other map includes all distribution points for citizens, temporary shelters, Red Cross and FEMA locations, as well as general go-to places. The Mapping Team organizes the information so that services for BOGs are easy for dispatchers to communicate and so that BOGs are easy to find.

Zello Help: Zello is a place where new volunteers, or anyone, can come to ask questions and get help about how to download and operate Zello. There are always people on Zello who can answer questions and provide direction.

The Social Media and Zello teams often make the first contact with survivors of disasters. These teams provide the public with information about where and how they can get the supplies and assistance they may need. They give direction to people in need during a chaotic time and can be a lifeline for those waiting to be rescued from a dire situation.

Volunteer Vetting: The Vetting Team interacts with people who have registered on CrowdRelief who want to volunteer. Team members call the potential volunteers to interview them. If they are a good fit, the Vetting Team has them sign an NDA and send a photo of their ID and of their license plate.

Volunteer Checklist:

- Sign up via link on CrowdRelief
- Sign NDA
- Review and sign SOP
- Send photos of ID and license plate
- Download apps: Zello, Zello channels, GPS/Tracking
- Arrive at staging location and check in
- Receive badge
- Check in with assigned team leader
- Respond to tickets as dispatched

Programs

We've developed three programs.

SAFE Camp: Swift Action Force Emergency Camp is a citizen command center and safe place established immediately following a disaster. Volunteers and nonprofits are able to work together there to meet the needs of survivors.

SAFE Camp is operated through a partnership with Walmart. We set up in a nearby Walmart store parking lot to provide food, water, clothes washing, medical and mental healthcare, and much more; collect and distribute supplies; and collaborate with nonprofits.

Community Caretakers: The mission of this program is to bring hope to individuals and help them regain a sense of control over their lives. Sometimes it means just giving a hug. That's what Ground Force Community Caretakers do. We stay behind after a disaster and assist with any kind of less-skilled labor that we can. We provide continuity for survivors and the greater disaster community.

Air Team: This program is made up of dispatch, logistics, technology, and marketing professionals who work remotely.

You won't see them on the ground or in our social media posts often, because their job is to provide critical information and oversight to the entire operation. They are in constant communication with our incident commanders, SAFE Camp director, and Community Caretakers. Listen for them and become an Air Team member by joining our public Zello channel, Cajun Navy Disaster Response. You can also register at https://volunteer.gocajunnavy.org.

Appendix B

What to Expect as a Volunteer

Expect the unexpected. Anything is possible when it comes to relief work, especially during the crisis. The best thing is to not have many expectations besides serving in any way that you are able. Sometimes it's intense, sometimes you just need to be there to listen, but make sure to find time to have fun, too.

Because relief work happens in a communal environment, volunteers make friends with other volunteers from all over the country. At times, you may be sleeping on an air mattress in a tent, and "showering" with bottled water, but this makes us realize our own capabilities! Expect that the experience will change, emotionally and physically, and you will come out stronger on the other end.

In times of disaster, community members who may have been strangers step up and help each other. It's the same in the volunteer community—you may be serving next to someone you never met, but you will share a life-changing experience together and will forever be bonded because of it.

There are days when our plans for relief work change, as the needs are always changing and the volunteers are coming and going, but we try our best to stay positive and meet the needs. The joy in the faces of the people we help is what keeps us motivated. When a community is vulnerable, any attention is valued. As a volunteer, you feel the connection and it can be really rewarding!

Community Support

Because we work based on the needs of the community, there is no "typical" workday. When disaster strikes, we may need to do rescues to make sure that community members are safe. From there, we work on cleanup and getting supplies to the community. Cleanup usually involves using chainsaws to clear tree debris from the roads and clearing the way for people to get in and out of their homes.

In the meantime, there may be volunteers who stay around the staffing area to receive and distribute donations. Some people are sent out on wellness checks or to deliver supplies directly to those who are in need but cannot get to us, usually elderly or disabled residents.

Other work includes cooking, serving food, organizing, tarping, running errands, documenting, handling social media, and much more!

We cannot guarantee the specific work you'll be doing, and there are always things that don't work out as planned, so we need individuals who are flexible and empathetic and can stay positive!

Food

The food is covered for the volunteers. Some days it's packed lunches out on the job; during the evenings we try to do communal dinners. Sometimes we have someone on duty who only does the cooking, and other times we coordinate amongst ourselves when we do group dinners. Individuals also have the opportunity to cook their own meals.

We try to make sure there are different options available in the communal pantry. Volunteers are able to bring their own food if they have specific foods they would like. Sometimes we eat canned foods because that is our only option, especially right after a storm. We also receive a lot of food via donations, so it depends what we are receiving.

Housing

Housing is provided for volunteers and can change, sometimes at a moment's notice. Right after a storm hits, we are usually staged in an outdoor space. Sometimes hotels will offer some rooms to our volunteers, and sometimes we are housed in a local business where we can store supplies and have a sleeping area and showers. We try to maintain communal space and private space, so volunteers can take a break from the group if they want.

Workday

Roles are assigned by your team leader. Groups keep in touch via Facebook and Zello. Debriefing will take place at the end of the day.

Downtime

This is time that we let the individual decide how to spend. Some like to be with other volunteers, and some enjoy alone time. During downtime, there is usually something the group is doing, whether it's playing cards or just getting to know each other. Some volunteers enjoy quiet activities such as reading books. Either way, volunteers should be free to "entertain" themselves after an intense day of helping the community. It is important for them to respect each other's time, energy, and need for privacy.

Quote

I find myself and others speaking of all the new things we learn and never realized we could do.

As volunteers, we accept the challenge to serve in whatever capacity we can, to the best of our ability and with love.

"We cannot guarantee anything except that we'll try." This is a quote I use all the time to be sure we under promise and over deliver.

Appendix C

Disaster Timeline

Louisiana Flooding (August 12-22, 2016)

The 2016 Louisiana flooding began as a four-day rain event without a name. The major rainstorm dumped four times the amount of water that is contained in Lake Pontchartrain, a 630-square-mile lake north of New Orleans. After the storm ended, floodwaters swelled all of the bayous, rivers, and creeks headed down to the Gulf of Mexico through South Louisiana. Over a ten-day period, 150,000 homes flooded.

People called 911, but the authorities were overwhelmed. Survivors turned to Facebook, frantically looking for help. We dispatched boaters to go find people who were texting us on Facebook from inside their attics. We began staging volunteers ahead of the imminent flooding to help us get to survivors more quickly. We emerged from this crisis with a new perspective on the value of technology.

In the media:

- Cajun Relief Foundation interview on American Family Radio about Louisiana flooding, AFRN, Oct 13 2016
- Cajun Navy's Global Disaster Initiative, *Weekends with Whitney*, Sep 25 2016
- Louisiana flooding's unsung heroes, Fox Business, Aug 25 2016
- Rob Gaudet interview on #BattlefieldLIVE, *Lantern Buzz*, Aug 20 2016

- Rob Gaudet interview about Louisiana flooding, *Hannity,* Aug 19 2016
- "Louisianians of the Year," *My New Orleans,* Jan 3 2017

Hurricane Harvey (August 23-30, 2017)

This devastating Category 4 hurricane made landfall in Texas and Louisiana, causing more than one hundred deaths. The Cajun Navy Ground Force responded with a spreadsheet, not dispatch software, logging more than 4,500 rescues. Our use of technology during a crisis would greatly improve with each disaster.

In the media:
- "The Cajun Relief Foundation Organized Thousands for the Cajun and Texas Navies, and They're Going Viral," American Military News, Sep 8 2017
- *Louisiana: The State We're In,* LPB, Sep 1 2017
- "Inspired by Cajun Navy, Texas Navy Volunteers Rescuing Houston Flood Victims," Fox Business, Aug 29 2017

Hurricane Irma (September 10-12, 2017)

Irma was considered the most intense hurricane to strike the continental United States since Katrina in 2005. In September of 2017, it resulted in 134 deaths and caused over $65 billion in damage. The northeastern Caribbean and Florida were the worst-hit areas. Marco Rubio called Cajun Navy Ground Force founder Rob Gaudet personally to ask him to organize citizen-led relief in Florida before the storm struck the state. When Irma made landfall, the Cajun Navy was waiting to help with forty-five teams in place.

In the media:
- "Taking the Cajun Navy Model to the Next Level in Helping Hurricane Victims," Fox Business, Sep 12 2017

- "Cajun Navy Wants to Help Florida After Hurricane Irma," *Miami Herald*, Sep 8 2017

Hurricane Maria (September 18, 2017)

Hurricane Maria struck just days after Hurricane Irma as a deadly Category 5 storm. It devastated the northeastern Caribbean in September 2017, particularly Dominica, St. Croix, and Puerto Rico. Maria is regarded as the worst natural disaster in recorded history to affect those islands. The Cajun Navy traveled over two thousand miles to help the people of Puerto Rico. Volunteers traveled to remote areas and distributed supplies to those in need, cut trees off of homes, tarped roofs, and assisted with recovery efforts.

Hurricane Florence (September 14, 2018)

Florence caused significant storm-surge flooding in parts of eastern North Carolina in advance of its landfall on September 14, 2018, and devastating freshwater flooding across much of the southeastern United States that lasted several days. The storm resulted in twenty-four direct and thirty indirect deaths. More than 70,000 structures were flooded by Hurricane Florence. The Cajun Navy Ground Force traveled more than 1,000 miles to provide relief for victims. We brought in supplies to areas that needed them most, and team members were able to assist in rescuing horses and other animals that were caught in floodwaters in Pender County, North Carolina. We provided an abundance of information connecting survivors with resources in the area.

In the media:
- "Charlotte Man Ready to Host First Responders Helping Hurricane Victims," WSOC-TV, Sep 13 2018

Hurricane Michael (October 10, 2018)

According to the National Hurricane Center, Hurricane Michael was directly responsible for sixteen deaths and about $25 billion in damage in the United States. Initially rated a top-end Category 4 when it made landfall, Michael was later upgraded to a Category 5 in post-analysis. Devastation from this storm was absolute, but the Cajun Navy delivered help to the people of Wewahitchka, Stone Mill Creek, and Dalkeith in the Florida Panhandle. The Cajun Navy Ground Force collaborated with other organizations for two supply drops. We also cut trees off of homes, tarped roofs, cleaned up yards, and did anything we could to help these hard-hit communities that other agencies had seemed to forget.

Tropical Storm Imelda (September 17, 2019)

Tropical Storm Imelda caused major flooding in southeast Texas. In After landfall, she continued to dump large amounts of rain on Texas and Louisiana. When Imelda's flooding hit in the early morning, 911 emergency lines were down. So the Cajun Navy Ground Force was soon bombarded with requests for rescue and other help. We coordinated our volunteers and delivered needed assistance and supplies.

In the media:
- "Cajun Navy Helps Residents in Texas amid Tropical Depression Imelda," BRProud.com, Sep 19, 2019

Hurricane Laura (August 26, 2020)

Hurricane Laura, a Category 4 hurricane, is tied with the 1856 Last Island hurricane and 2021's Hurricane Ida as the strongest recorded storm to directly strike Louisiana, as measured by maximum sustained winds. Laura slammed into the Cajun heartland in August 2020. Cajun Navy Ground Force founder Rob Gaudet jumped into action days before the storm hit in preparation for the impending destruction that would come to Lake Charles. The Cajun Navy prepared and served meals in the weeks following Laura. They distributed supplies, cleared roads, cut trees off of houses, and tarped homes— continuing to assist the citizens of Lake Charles however they could. Our team has not wavered and is still there, helping with ongoing recovery efforts.

In the media:
- "Technology Plays Key Role in Cajun Navy Volunteer Efforts," *American Press,* Jan 6 2021
- "Cajun Navy Group Continues to Coordinate Volunteers, Supplies after Storms," KATC, Nov 12 2020
- "Cajun Navy Continues Disaster Relief Efforts in Lake Charles," KNOE, Sep 9 2020
- "Cajun Navy Gives Out Hot Meals in Downtown Lake Charles," KPLC, Sep 3 2020
- *Hurricane Laura & The Cajun Navy,* Confluence documentary, Sep 1 2020
- "Volunteer Rescue Groups Prepare Equipment in Case of Flooding, Extreme Wind Event," Click2Houston.com, Aug 22 2020

Hurricane Delta (October 8, 2020)

Hurricane Delta was the fourth named storm to strike Louisiana in 2020 and the tenth to make landfall in the United States. Delta hit Creole, Louisiana as a Category 2 hurricane on Thursday, October 8 with winds of 100 miles per hour. She weakened to a Category 1 as she moved inland, causing widespread power cuts. The National Hurricane Center also warned of an eight-foot-high "life-threatening storm surge" across the Louisiana coast, caused by high winds from Delta.

In the media:
- "Resident Recalls Being Rescued from Floodwaters

during Hurricane Delta," KPLC, Oct 12 2020
- "Storm-Ravaged Southwestern Louisiana Takes Stock of Damage after Delta," *Washington Post*, Oct 10 2020
- "Cajun Navy Ready to Help ahead of Second Hurricane in 6 weeks," WAPT, Oct 9 2020
- "Rattled Louisiana Gulf Coast Slammed by Hurricane Delta," *Washington Post*, Oct 9 2020

North American Winter Storm—Ice Storms in Louisiana and Texas (February 13-17, 2021)

This storm had impacts from Canada to Mexico. It began in the Pacific Northwest and quickly moved into the South. It moved on to the Midwestern and Northeastern United States after that. It caused blackouts for almost 10 million people in Mexico and the US, especially in Texas.

In the media:
- "Cajun Navy Distributes Bottled Water in Beaumont," 12News.com, Feb 22 2021
- "Cajun Navy Reaching Out to Help Texans in Need," Click2Houston.com, Feb 18 2021
- "Cajun Navy Volunteers Assist SWLA with Cold-Weather Supplies," KPLC, Feb 11 2021